QUANT BY QUANT

THE AUTOBIOGRAPHY OF
MARY QUANT

V&A Publishing

First published by Cassell & Co. Ltd, 1966
This edition published by V&A Publishing, 2018
Victoria and Albert Museum
South Kensington
London SW7 2RL
www.vam.ac.uk/info/publishing

Distributed in North America by Abrams,
an imprint of ABRAMS

E-book edition
ISBN 978 1 85177 668 9

Paperback edition
ISBN 978 1 85177 958 1

10 9 8 7 6 5 4 3 2 1
2022 2021 2020 2019 2018

A catalogue record for this book is available from
the British Library.

Cover illustration © Beatriz Lostalé 2018

Printed and bound by CPI Group (UK) Ltd, Croydon

V&A Publishing

Supporting the world's leading
museum of art and design,
the Victoria and Albert
Museum, London

To Tony Quant

FOREWORD

Life was a whizz! It was such fun and unexpectedly wonderful despite, or perhaps because of its intensity. We were so fortunate with our enormous luck and timing; we partied too – there were no real boundaries.

I relished the early experiences: the garments were audacious, daring and risqué. I wanted them to be eye-catching, strong and colourful, to offer freedom for the young, to take them straight from work to an evening out – totally unlike the way our mothers looked. Previously accepted rules had become totally irrelevant to modern day living and I loved the way that everyone had the opportunity to make their way in their chosen field, irrespective of their background.

It all seemed to happen at once: planning for up to two years ahead, enjoying the reaction to collections featuring fabrics chosen almost 18 months previously, reviewing the impact (good and bad) of previous designs; there was constant confusion about which time frame one was dealing with.

The business grew so quickly. Once we started it seemed we never stopped, travelling breathlessly from London to Newcastle or New York, to Paris, Turin or Tokyo, and there were always new ideas, fresh inspirations and experiences; contrasting things to see and assimilate because fashion is all about change. The revolutionary cosmetics, the tights which enabled the mini skirt to be even shorter, all the accessories – we swung from one demand to the next a dozen times a day.

The feeling of verve and zest was everywhere. It drove the ideas, the excitement, the compulsion to do more, reach out and touch all those whose lives embraced the new liberation, to demonstrate the differences between post-war Britain and the frenzied period that the '60s became. We even changed the way that clothes were shown, with the models dancing to rock music, which was completely different.

The explosion of energy, generating and reflecting the change of social attitudes, tore through music, design and art, photography, film, architecture, theatre and the 'shocking' plays and drama which influenced the press and television programmes of the day. It was a new world and fashion was at its centre. Fashion was becoming more democratic and we spearheaded the changes in retailing that seem so familiar today. There was such a sense of freedom, old restraints were being swept away, pushing barriers, breaking rules. I wanted to provide fashion for everyone.

Like most happy times it all passed too quickly but the future is for the young and it always will be.

Mary Quant

2018

QUANT BY QUANT

Life as I know it now began for me when I first saw Plunket.

I had to wait three months before he noticed me and during that time I just watched from the outskirts of a posse of disciples who surrounded him constantly, hanging on his words, rushing about to fetch and carry for him and generally imitating his style.

I had been at the Goldsmiths' College in south-east London for a few months when Plunket turned up, ostensibly to study Illustration although I should think the records of his attendance at classes must be unique because he never seemed to make an appearance until late in the afternoon.

Apparently he used Goldsmiths' as a club and it was only when he was pushed and had nothing better to do that he turned up at all. So long as he dropped in and continued to be registered as a student, his mother gave him an allowance.

His arrival had an enormous effect on everybody. He really was quite something. To begin with, there was his appearance. He was very lean and long. He seemed to have no clothes of his own. He wore his mother's pyjama tops as shirts, generally in that colour known as 'old gold' which usually comes – as they say in the trade we're now in – in shantung.

His trousers also came out of his mother's wardrobe. Beautifully cut and very sleek fitting, the zip was at the side and they were in weird and wonderful variations of purple, prune, crimson and putty. The trouble was that they came to a stop half-way down the calf of the leg so there was always a wide gap of white flesh between the tops of the Chelsea-type boots he wore and the end of the trouser legs.

I found out later that the dramatic effect his appearance created on us at the College was absolutely unintentional. He did most of his growing between fifteen and sixteen when he suddenly shot up about six inches. His mother was ill at the time and she simply hadn't noticed.

Apart from the visual impact he made on us all, he also managed to create the impression that he was immensely rich. He lived in Chelsea; he had a house all to himself because his mother was convalescing in the country; he played jazz on the trumpet; was thought to take drugs; and boasted the wildest parties in London.

It must have been after one of these parties that he was seen to produce a five-pound note from his pocket ... something enormously impressive. And he carried a film script around with the most important-looking cover ... the words 'film script' written all over it in the boldest, blackest, biggest type.

He was the most bizarre and worldly and advanced, fanciful and fantastic character I had ever dreamed of. I thought of him as a great film star, an impression heightened by these henchmen who were always with him and who could be heard saying, 'Yes, Plunket' ... 'No, Plunket' ... 'Can I get anything for you, Plunket?' ... 'Have you got your script, Plunket?' ... 'How's it going, Plunket?' The film script he carried around was *Tom Brown's Schooldays* for which he had had a screen test and been short-listed. However, he did not get the part.

I never found the courage to speak to him and it wasn't until the Christmas Ball, a fancy dress affair rather like a smaller and more parochial version of the old Chelsea Arts Ball, at the end of his first term at Goldsmiths' that he noticed me.

Because I was small, I had been stuck on top of a pile of balloons and, at midnight, practically naked, perched in the middle of hundreds of them, I was dragged round the dance floor on a float. I clutched an enormous bunch of balloons round my middle to disguise as much of myself as I could as I was rather fat.

This was the moment when Alexander says he first saw me. But, even then, he didn't speak. He was having a slightly unsatisfactory evening. He had arrived most immaculately dressed as Oscar Wilde, wearing a superb black frock-coat and carrying a single enormous lily. The trouble was that another student turned up as Lord Alfred Douglas. They were made to dance together all evening.

Having missed his chance to speak to me at the Goldsmiths' hop, Alexander says now that he had to make a terrific effort at the beginning of the next term to pluck up the courage to accost me.

From the moment we did speak to each other, it was a whizz. We started doing everything together. I didn't give up all my old boy friends at once. It was simply that gradually they became obsolete. And the same sort of thing happened with Alexander.

When we first met he had a girl friend who was known as his 'fiancée'. They had been great friends during his last year at Bryanston. She was at the sister school, Critchell, and they had spent most of their last summer term together.

Bryanston is a sort of mock Eton except that the boys there seem to have an extraordinary amount of freedom. Alexander was supposed to be doing 'Art' during his last year there but so far as I can make out his school attendances became simply a matter of clocking in at church once a week.

In spite of this, he is still very much in favour of a public school education as he says that if you're not very clever, you can get by better if you've either been to a public school or come from the East End.

Plunket used to make me frantically jealous by telling me how beautiful his fiancée was … what a wonderful, 'bony' face she had … the face of a great model, he'd say. And how madly attractive he found her proud, sensitive nostrils. I said she looked like a horse in a panic!

Fortunately – for me – she grew in height even faster than Alexander and when they were both around fifteen, she was two inches taller than he was which didn't please him at all. By the time he had caught up and hit six foot two – which happened within the next couple of years – she was at university and he had become acclimatized to the mad world we managed to create at Goldsmiths'.

At sixteen, both Alexander and I thought of ourselves as pretty advanced. Most of our friends were older than we were. This was probably inevitable then. We were living in our own environment but sharing it with others not only older but with far greater experience of life.

It was not so long after the end of the war and quite a number of the students at Goldsmiths' had spent several years in the forces before they got the chance to complete their education.

We were tremendously keen to keep up with these older people and our main object was to give the impression that we knew a great deal more about life than we really did. This wasn't

5

too difficult for Plunket with his house in Chelsea and his reputation. He was always streets ahead of anyone else. When it came to decadence, it was always he who got the best ideas and had it all worked out to the last detail and was in full charge of the operation. The way he would spend all day in bed, getting up around four in the afternoon and staying up all night doing the rounds of the jazz clubs, seemed to us splendidly cosmopolitan and advanced.

But, for me, the next few years were rather like a nightmare in stupefying Technicolor. There was all the tremendous fun, the terrific parties and fantastic excitement closely intermingled with the terrifying rows at home and the appalling family scenes which became almost a part of the daily routine.

I suppose I was trying to have the best of all worlds. I felt I must get my Diploma for my parents' sake and because it meant so much to them. I had to be up every morning at seven to get to the College on time. All the same I wasn't prepared to sacrifice my evenings with Plunket and these were frustrating, too, because when he arrived completely fresh and raring to go after a day in bed, I had done a day's work.

Worse than this, when the evening really got going, I would have to leave to catch the last train that would get me home by 11 p.m., the deadline set by my father. I seldom made it and all the way home I would have to steel myself for the row which I knew was bound to come the moment I stepped inside the door.

It wasn't my parents' fault. They were terribly worried about the life I was leading. My brother Tony and I have always been a worry to them largely because neither of us has inherited their ability to concentrate on work to the exclusion of all else. For so long as I can remember, there has always been a certain amount of tension in our home because of this.

It was only with the greatest difficulty that I ever persuaded them to allow me to go to art school. They wanted me to be a teacher. The fashion world, which was my aim, was far too chancy for them. It was only when I managed to win a scholarship to Goldsmiths' that I was able to persuade them to agree to a compromise ... if they would allow me to go to Goldsmiths', I would take the Art Teachers' Diploma.

The way we look on life these days, their outlook on careers is, perhaps, a little narrow. They recognize only professional qualifications; they worship the sort of qualifications that come from the passing of exams. To them, these are a sort of insurance against the future ... something permanently behind you to fall back on if need be. The system they recognize insists on exam passes. Every single child has to be geared to exams. Consequently they are turned out like jellies from the same mould. Such a system nips originality in the bud. Not that my parents ever wanted either Tony or me to be original.

At home it was a sort of sin to sit around doing nothing ... both of us were made to feel we ought to be swotting for something or other all the time. We did, in fact, manage to have terrific fun but we had a feeling of guilt about it. And it was only when I went to Goldsmiths' that, for the first time in my life, I realized that there are people who give their lives to the pursuit of pleasure and indulgence of every kind in preference to work. At first it was a shock even to me; to my parents, such a thing was incomprehensible.

Nothing that had gone before in their lives had conditioned them to an understanding of the kind of life these people led and which I, at this time, wanted to live. They hated Plunket before they ever met him. They hated the influence he had on me and the sort of life he led. It was impossible for them to understand anything of the strange, fast-moving world of uninhibited language and behaviour which was then his natural background. It was – and still is – impossible for them to understand anyone who puts fun first and everything else far down the line.

To them, work has always come first ... it had to. Security has come to them through hard work ... and more hard work ... to the exclusion of everything else in life. And – to them – there is only one definition of hard work ... studying books, passing exams and getting distinguished letters after your name.

My family has none of the hereditary advantages of Plunket's.

Both my father and mother have always been tremendously ambitious for my brother and for me. They have brought the family a long way from the mining villages of their parents; they desperately want us to take it still further. Even in our earliest schooldays, it was instilled into us that it is never good enough to come second or third or fourth, however strong the competition. To be first is the one thing that matters.

To have any understanding of their feelings during the quite awful time they must have gone through during my years at art school, you must know something of my family background. Both my mother and father are Welsh. My mother was born in Kidwelly, my father in Merthyr. They grew up surrounded by the hardships and deprivations of the mining communities during the twenties and early thirties and I realize, now that I am older, what tremendous courage and determination they must have had to have accomplished all they have done entirely by their own efforts.

From their local schools, they went on to grammar school and from there to Cardiff University. Every step forward was made possible by their own scholarship. They were born with good brains and they have never stopped using and improving them. Both got Firsts at university and both have dedicated their lives to teaching. The persistent habit of hard work is so ingrown in them now that to do less than work hard, always, all the time, is a mortal sin.

Schooldays would probably have been pretty awful for Tony and me had it not been for the war. The war disrupted our education as it did everything else. Almost my first clear memory is the day we were evacuated from Blackheath (where we were born) to a village in Kent. As both my mother and father were teachers, we were sent as a family. My father was in charge of the party.

When we arrived at this village we were lined up on the village green and split up into age groups, rather like cattle being sorted out into little pens on a market day. The local people walked all round the green, carefully inspecting each child before making a selection. It must have been awful for those children who were away from home and alone for the first time. For Tony and me it was different because we had our parents with us and we knew we were not going to be separated from them. We followed the local people round listening to their conversation and giggling together when we heard them saying to each other such things as 'He's got good muscles … he's strong enough to work on the farm … he's a healthy-looking child – let's have him!'

Tony was about five at the time, very small, very skinny and half-starved-looking. He had a little white face with an angelic smile and rather long dark red hair. He was the sort of child people would look at, shake their heads sadly and mutter, 'He won't last long. He'll never live to grow up. Poor little thing!'

Of course my mother knew … we all knew … he was as tough as hell. He had the most enormous appetite and would fight boys twice his size.

Whilst my father and mother were rushing round trying to arrange the right billeting for all the children in their care, Tony was strolling round absolutely lapping up all the admiration he was getting. The women surrounded him and I could hear them saying, 'Oh, he's sweet. We must have him. Poor child. You can see he's been starved!'

And they'd dig in their shopping baskets and produce apples and sweets and sometimes a piece of chocolate. He was the hit of the whole thing and over and over again women had to be told that he was not for billeting … he was one of a family. We were, in fact, a sort of job lot. As my father was going to teach the children from London, we had to be taken as one unit.

Eventually when all the others were settled and had been taken off to their billets, my father was told that we were to stay in one of the big houses on the outskirts of the village. It was really rather a nice house with a lovely garden. The trouble was that the people who owned it had never had any children of their own and were terrified of us from the start. They were slightly eccentric and obviously on the verge of a bad case of war hysteria. Everything that came into the house was hoarded. If we'd been allowed only one ounce of tea and sugar a week, half of it would have been hidden away.

Trouble was inevitable even if Tony and I had been the quietest and best behaved children in the world, which we were not. As it was, within a short time, the woman who owned the house was on the verge of a nervous breakdown. She became hysterical at the sight of us and everything that went wrong in the house or in the garden was always our fault. When the chickens started to lay eggs without shells, we were responsible. It was our red hair … we had put a jinx on the chickens.

After we'd survived the chickens episode, it was the apples. Some of the best Cox's Orange Pippins in the orchard had disappeared. We were forbidden ever to pick an apple again. It just so happened that we hadn't in fact been picking the apples and the false accusation upset Tony so much that I believe he thought of nothing else for days. Then he had a brilliant brainwave; when everyone else in the house was busy, we'd go into the orchard, climb the trees and eat the apples we wanted without picking them. 'We only promised we wouldn't *pick* them,' he kept emphasizing.

We really put our hearts into this … it was days before we were discovered. Poor woman! It must have been a ghastly experience for her when she walked into the orchard to count her precious apples and found nothing left but cores hanging on the trees.

This was the summer before the Battle of Britain started; it was a marvellous one for us because we were living in the country for the first time and we had so much freedom. Our parents were so busy getting the other children established in their new homes and fixing their schooling that we were left pretty much to our own devices. That whole summer we didn't go to school.

One of the things my father and the other teachers had to do was to arrange walks and games and outings that would keep the children from London amused out of school hours and so out of mischief. We were included in all these activities (I suspect my father wanted to keep his eye on us as much as he possibly could) and, because Tony and I were so much smaller and younger than the older boys for whom he was directly responsible, we were utterly spoilt.

I was the only girl and I was allowed to join in everything. I was even taught to play cricket. Tony was adopted as the school mascot and this meant that we were taken on all sorts of wonderful expeditions. When we got tired, there was always someone willing to carry us the rest of the way.

We had a splendid summer.

September came and with it the Battle of Britain really started. Possibly the powers-that-be must have realized then what a jolly silly place they had sent us to. We were in the direct line of the enemy planes passing over the coast on their way to London. West Malling was practically the centre of their cross-country run. We had a grandstand view of the enemy's campaign of attack and because we had no understanding of the grim tragedies of war, this was tremendous fun.

It was all too much for the poor couple we'd been billeted on. In any case, my parents were feeling the strain of living in someone else's house with two children who were never out of trouble. They started searching for some sort of alternative place to live and eventually they were lucky enough to get a bungalow vacated by some nervous people who couldn't bear the sound of the enemy engines overhead. Built high up on a hill, it had the most magnificent view overlooking the countryside of Kent towards the coast.

It couldn't have been a better vantage point for supervising the enemy's activities. A look-out had been built for the Home Guard just above our bungalow on the hill. But it was never manned full time. We took it over. We organized a sort of posse of local children and we'd all meet at this look-out and spend most of the day there waiting for the Nazis to come over. We had bicycles and as soon as we saw a plane crash, we would set off at full speed to find it. Very often we managed to get there before the police or the Home Guard and it wasn't long before we were all quite experienced looters. We took everything we could apart from the plane itself. We would have had this too if we'd been able to move it. We acquired machine guns which were kept under our beds, goggles, flying helmets, whole chunks of aeroplanes ... in fact, anything we could carry and get away with quickly. Our prize possession was some poor pilot's thumb which had been shot off and which we carefully preserved in vinegar in an airtight bottle.

One day when we got to a plane that had just been shot down we found the German pilot alive and conscious. We solemnly stood around him and arrested him. Poor chap, he could do nothing about it; his back was broken. I think he must have been numb with shock and concussion because he gave no sign of being in pain. He talked quite naturally – he spoke very good English – and after we'd said silly things like 'You're our prisoner!' 'We're arresting you!' he told us about life in Germany in the friendliest way.

This sort of wild life couldn't go on for ever of course. The day came when Tony and I were taken to the village school. This was the day when Tony and I really ganged up; when the close relationship which exists between us started to develop.

For as long as I can remember, we have always been pretty close. We learned young that we would have to stand up for each other and preserve a united front if we were going to get away with anything in our family. We had a solemn pact whereby we were sworn to protect each other at all costs … to lie in our teeth for each other … back up any alibi … support each other through any crisis. There were many times when we fought like two outrageous little boys; we were always battling but if anyone else attacked either one, we would turn on that person as one, absolutely solid.

Being school teachers, and particularly at this time when they were responsible for so many children away from their own homes, my mother and father were both pretty severe with us. They had to practise at home what they preached at school and so far as possible we were kept heavily under the thumb. Tony and I were treated exactly the same. It was made absolutely clear to both of us from the start that we would have to earn our own livings. My parents never even considered the possibility that marriage might be a way out for girls. I was made terribly aware that it was entirely my own responsibility to make a success of my life. I feel sure that the one good thing that developed out of my parents' uncompromising attitude was the unusually close bond between Tony and me.

We started our school lives together. To our surprise we were given a great welcome by the other children. It seemed as if we were expected to take charge and organize such villainies as the local children could never have thought out themselves. Maybe it was just because we came from the great big City; maybe the children had overheard their parents talking of the things we got up to. Whatever it was, it wasn't long before we managed to stir up a certain amount of havoc. We were moved to another school. Much the same sort of thing happened here. We were moved on again.

This time we were lucky. We found ourselves in the really old-fashioned type of village school which I can't believe exists any longer. It was little more than a one-room shack, with a couple of dilapidated oil stoves for heating in the winter. There was only one teacher who was called 'Governess' or 'Gov'. She was the most wonderful woman and a brilliant teacher. In this one-room shack we sat with children of all ages ... the kindergarten at one end of the room, fourteen-year-olds at the other.

Goodness, what I learned from Gov. I am sure she taught me far more than anyone else in the time I was in her schoolroom. She seemed to us to be immensely old. I think she was quite old because she had been called back from retirement to carry on through the war. She had complete control of every child in the room. She would spend the whole day going round from one child to the next, giving out work, correcting work, helping, teaching. She always carried a ruler and anyone who slacked off or started talking or even began to look like mischief, would get a sharp tap on the knuckles. From Gov this was quite enough. She never had any trouble with boys or girls of any age. She was the sort of person who inspires obedience.

Then – as so often happens – people in high places who knew nothing about Gov or the wonderful little centre of learning she had created, started writing to the local Press and agitating about the shocking conditions of the old school shack. On the surface it must have appeared totally inadequate for any kind of education; it would have been without Gov.

These people must have agitated pretty effectively because in a short time one of the rare modern schools built in war-time went up nearby. Gov was retired once more. In her place, a new headmistress was installed – very modern like the building and very advanced. She was so advanced that she wore purple corduroy bermuda shorts and had her hair cut like a man's. She was the direct opposite of Gov. And she had no ability to keep any kind of discipline at all.

Looking back now, I realize that this was an advanced school so far as sex went. We were allowed to go to school in bathing suits during the hot weather, the idea being that if boys and girls saw enough of each other they would not be interested. It wasn't true of course.

I don't know whether the headmistress ever thought as deeply as this … probably not. She was fully occupied organizing the situation because she was so short of staff. She had to arrange for other teachers to take her own classes. Everyone moved up one. This appeared to work splendidly until it was realized that it created a gap at the bottom. The kindergarten was without a mistress. There was no one to teach the babies.

For some unknown reason, I was told to do this. I can only imagine it was because my parents were teachers. They were never consulted and had no idea of the way in which I was spending my time at school. And I made sure they didn't find out for as long as possible. Teaching the babies was much more fun than doing lessons.

My class came under the heading of 'Mixed Infants' and I took them in all subjects. Perhaps there may be something in heredity. Anyway, I found no great difficulty in taking my classes. It all seemed to come quite naturally. From earliest days, Tony and I had played schools. We had always been able to find bits of real chalk in my father's pockets and we had been allowed to use old exercise books – the real ones with the multiplication tables on the back. Teaching the 'Mixed Infants' was to me an exciting continuation of a game I had played for years. My own education stopped completely though I suspect I was absorbing more than

I knew from the books I had to read up before taking the babies in spelling or geography or history.

It couldn't go on for ever. It was only a question of time before my parents found out. They were terribly shocked; and indignant; and furious.

At what must have been an enormous expense for them and a great sacrifice, they took me away and packed me off to a boarding-school near Tunbridge Wells ... a very proper, very correct, absolutely heartless establishment.

This school was chosen because although there was proper accommodation for full-time boarders, it also took additional day pupils who couldn't afford the full boarding fees and who were able to live, by arrangement, at a local boarding-house.

I was one of the cut-rate pupils and found myself in the sort of dreary *pension* where they call lodgers 'paying guests'. It was full of old ladies and not-so-old ladies all living there more or less permanently for the duration of the war.

I soon found out how smart the owners were. By taking some of the girls from the school, they were able to get our full rations but we were given only margarine, never butter. And never meat. All the butter and meat went to the old ladies who were prepared to pay very well indeed for such extras.

It struck me as an extremely bright idea and, so far as I could find out, it seemed to work well. This was my first introduction to Big Business.

For the first time in my life I was regimented. I was no longer an individual. I very soon lost all identity. I was miserable ... desperately lonely and utterly wretched. I missed Tony. I was so unhappy. I couldn't cry and I used to envy the girls who could give way to tears and howl and howl and never stop howling until their parents were sent for and they were taken away. I longed for my parents to come and take me away but I dared not tell them how much I hated the place.

Then – luckily for me – the bombing started all over again and in real earnest. It was impossible to ignore what a danger zone the countryside of Kent had become. My father and his school were transferred to Wales. It was the answer to my unspoken prayers. I knew my mother would never leave me in Tunbridge Wells if she was going to Wales.

I have never departed from any place more thankfully than I left my first – and last – boarding-school.

Once again, summer was on the way. The term had already started when we arrived in Wales with my mother. Tony and I had another summer off. We had the sea and the sands and the fishing boats. We also had freedom. It seemed too good to be true.

It didn't take Tony and me long to discover that quite a lot of people who appeared to us to be extremely rich visited places on the coast around Tenby where we were. Successful business men would deposit their wives and families there for the whole summer and come down for week-ends and whenever they could get time off. They were the sort of chaps who think the great thing is to sail.

Tony and I would watch them arrive with their super little sailing dinghies. We knew in advance exactly what would happen. The next morning, we'd see them put the dinghy in the water and it was only at that moment that they would realize it isn't all that easy to sail any craft round a coast like Pembrokeshire's.

We decided to go into business.

Already we had made a number of friends among the local fishermen. It didn't take us long to persuade them to teach us how to handle a boat and we were constantly on the water anyway with the local children who knew all about it.

We set up as a sort of advisory bureau. Whenever some rich-looking family arrived we would let them know, one way or another, that we were experts and free to give sailing lessons. They'd fall for it nearly every time. The super new sailing dinghy would be handed over to us and we'd give lessons to members of the family in turn. We worked out a carefully regulated scale of charges.

Frequently we would be asked to sail a family who wanted an all-day picnic round the coast to one of the nearby rocky and picturesque bays. Pembrokeshire is a marvellous piece of coastline. We would leave them there for the day with their expensive-looking picnic baskets and beach balls and swimming gear and come back to pick them up again after tea to sail home. In the meantime, it was part of the arrangement that we should have full use of their boat.

I forget exactly how our charges worked out but I know we did quite well. So well, in fact, that we were soon able to hire a much bigger boat with a diesel engine and run organized day trips round the coast.

It was all terrific fun and very profitable.

Then we extended the business still further. We started an agency to clean up the boats at the end of the holiday and put them on the train back to wherever they'd come from. This paid well too.

On the days when the weather was too bad to do any sailing and I had to stay at home, I was sewing. I think I always knew that what I wanted to do most of all was to make clothes … clothes that would be fun to wear. As a very small child, I had idolized a little girl we knew who took tap dancing lessons and wore very skinny black sweaters, short black pleated skirts and long black tights, white ankle socks and black patent ankle strap shoes. She had the sort of fringe now favoured by Vidal Sassoon. How I envied her!

I grew up in a state of continual embarrassment because of the way I was dressed. I still remember every dress I had as a child. I hated them all except the few I managed, surreptitiously, to alter. I hated being forced to wear my cousin's cast-off clothes which were much too ornate for me.

When I was about six and in bed with measles, I spent one night cutting up the bedspread – a sort of family heirloom that belonged to an aunt – with nail scissors. Even at that age I could see that the wild colour of the bedspread would make a super dress.

I was determined that one day I would choose my own kind of clothes. I knew clothes would be the great interest of my life. But all the time I was growing up it did not occur to me that I could earn a living from something that was so much fun.

The only reason I was encouraged to sew at all was an eco-nomic one. Obviously it was a saving if I could alter my clothes as I grew out of them. And these were the days of make-do and mend anyway. I was helped, too, because, with clothing coupons, very few schools insisted on any precise school uniform. I promptly jumped on this and invented a uniform all my own.

The first time I had any real success with this was at Tenby. My mother had had to buy for me two or three blue and white check gingham dresses when I went to the boarding-school in Tunbridge Wells. They were the usual type of shapeless schoolgirls' things, cut with so much room for growth that they didn't fit anywhere and had to be tied round the middle to hold them together. When we got to Tenby, I unpicked these dresses and made them into the sort of dresses I liked ... terribly short and chic and very *à la* Bardot with tremendously full flared skirts. I wore boys' white knee socks with them. I was able to get away with this because I said it was the uniform I'd had to wear at my last school. I was the envy of all the other girls!

Fortunately we had an old sewing machine at home which had once belonged to an aunt and I had been taught the elementary principles of sewing in class at school.

I will never forget the first thing I made.

With terrific care and worry and love and all the rest of it, I embroidered a pyjama case for my mother. It was to be her Christmas present. The day came and with great excitement I handed her the parcel.

I watched her open it. She was thrilled with it. After she had done the pleasure bit and all that and everyone had admired my work, I suddenly realized that she was trying to put her hand inside the case and it wouldn't go. It was agonizing. I had embroidered it right through from front to back.

As far back as I can remember, I loved sewing. And I was always tremendously interested in what people wore. As a child, it used to worry me why grown-ups always insisted on wearing gloves. I couldn't understand why they always put on high heels for dancing and made such a thing of matching shoes and handbag.

I think one of my current fashion hates grew out of this. I can't bear over-accessorization ... a white hat worn with white gloves, white shoes and a white umbrella. I used to be told, over and over again, that a redhead – as I was then – should always wear green.

I used to ask why? No one ever gave me a satisfactory answer. Eventually I decided that such rules were totally irrelevant to modern day living. Rules are invented for lazy people who don't want to think for themselves.

When our first summer at Tenby came to an end, Tony and I were sent to the Tenby County School. I loved this school. This was a thoroughly happy time for us all but, like most happy times, it passed too quickly.

News came that my father's school was to move back to London and he had to go with the boys. My mother stayed with us and we had a few more months on the coast I love. Discipline broke down a bit in my father's absence and Tony and I were able to lead a fairly wild life. Tony used to be terribly naughty at times. But, naughty as he was, he must have been a much more satisfactory child to my parents than I was.

He was always very bright and never had any difficulty with exams. The thought of exams reduced me to a state of terror. I would get myself thoroughly worked up days beforehand and when the time came, I'd be mentally exhausted. I used to study dementedly and then find I couldn't remember anything.

Tony was different. He'd swot like mad up to about four or five days before the actual examination. Then he would just play tennis or go to the movies; go to bed early and sleep soundly. He would sit the examination in a perfectly healthy and relaxed state so of course he always passed well.

One of my troubles was that I never knew which were my best subjects. Every school I went to – and there were so many I don't really remember how many – assessed my abilities differently. At one school I would have no great difficulty in coming top in maths; in the next, I would be consistently bottom; at one I would be told I was good at art; at the next that I had no talent at all. I think probably this – and the fact that I was so often in disgrace at home for indifferent results and far-from-good school reports – had the effect of undermining any confidence I might have had in myself.

When we were all back together in our own home in Shooter's Hill near Blackheath, my mother was able to renew contact with those friends and relations we had been out of touch with because of the war. And it was at this time that I came to know Auntie Frances, one of my father's sisters, really well. She had always fascinated me. In my teens, she fascinated me still more. She began to have more and more influence on my life.

Looking back, I realize that Auntie Frances must have caused quite a lot of trouble in my home ... she absolutely adored my father and was always rather possessive about him ... but she had such a tremendous personality that it was impossible for my mother to refuse to have her when she wrote asking if she could stay with us.

I had two single beds in my room at home and Auntie Frances persuaded my mother to let her share my room. I was delighted because she was one of the few grown-ups with the sense to talk to a child in precisely the same way as she would talk to someone of her own age.

She loved talking and she would talk most of the night. I don't know when she slept. I do know that when I simply couldn't keep awake any longer, she would get up and go downstairs. Quite often she would spend the night rearranging the furniture in the living-room and she would even take pieces of furniture from one room to another. It must have been infuriating for my mother. She would go downstairs in the morning and find the whole of the downstairs had been fixed in a new way during the night.

Another nerve-racking eccentricity of hers was to go shopping on the grand scale. A large sale notice in any window was irresistible to her. She would buy the most awful dud stock ... it might be some extraordinary Art Nouveau drapery or a ghastly Turkish carpet ... and she would order this to be delivered to my parents' home. It was bad enough being loaded with this terrible stuff; worse when my father received the bill.

All this meant nothing to me. To me, she remained completely fascinating. She was small with dark, dark hair and dark brown, penetrating eyes that seemed to go right through you. She had arthritis so she was rather lame in one leg and always used a stick. When she came back into our bedroom in the early hours of the morning after one of her nocturnal expeditions downstairs, the sound of her stick would awaken me and sometimes I would see her walking round and round my bed, mumbling strange things and moving her arms and hands and stick round in the air. It would have been very frightening if I had not been so devoted to her.

One night I asked her why she did it and she told me she had a premonition that she would die and she wanted to make sure that she could pass on to me the strange powers she knew she possessed. She was a spiritualist and a professional medium. She used to hold seances and would tell me all about these in great detail. She told me about my grandparents who died before I was born and after she had been in touch with them in the spirit world, she told me in tremendous detail the course my life would follow.

Everything she said then has steadily come true over the years to date. She told me that I would design clothes and that I would influence people; that I would travel the world. She mentioned by name the countries I would visit and told me those in which my name would become famous; she told me all about Alexander long before I met him; where we would meet and how it would work out. She said that Alexander would inherit a small amount of capital and that it was this that would give us a start; she foretold the sort of relationship we would have and the influence we would have on each other. She was absolutely accurate about his character. One thing she repeated over and over again, 'You will have to grow up together.'

She warned me of my own weaknesses and told me how I would have to fight these and overcome them. And she said I would end up colossally rich!

She was incredibly accurate about Tony, too. She said our parents should stop worrying about him ... he would pass all his exams with honours; that his work would bring him in close contact with women (he is, in fact, a dental surgeon and a cosmetic surgeon, too) and that one day he would invent something of tremendous value.

When she died, I was in the middle of a mad love affair with a man at least twice my age who seemed to me then to be absolutely super and marvellous and extremely elegant and worldly.

I was mad about this man. I had had various boy friends of my own age before but this was something quite different. I really hero-worshipped him.

The trouble was that I knew he was having an affair with a woman of his own age and looking back now it is quite obvious that, to him, I was just an amusing side-line interest. I was desperately jealous of this woman. I envied everything about her, even her name, which was Daisy. I wished I had been called it.

To me, she was terrific. She had a marvellous figure and always looked tremendously elegant and well groomed and sophisticated. She had enormous influence on me. I studied her and I tried to copy her.

She was better at tennis than I was which was maddening because I thought I was quite good after all the hours I had spent acting more or less as a batting board for Tony to practise against. She looked super on the courts wearing boys' shorts. I used to stand for hours watching her, working myself up into an absolute frenzy of jealousy. It got worse and worse. It became almost an all-consuming passion. I loathed her and over and over again I wished her dead. I was in a permanent rage because, of course, I couldn't really compete in any way. She was so far ahead of me in everything.

One Friday evening I was at the tennis club watching her play and I kept saying to myself, 'I wish you were dead! I wish you were dead!'

The next day, she was. It was ghastly. I suppose she must have been in her early thirties. I was told she had appendicitis. Anyway, she simply dropped dead. It was so sudden it was unbelievable. I was convinced it was my fault. This was it! This was the power Auntie Frances had bequeathed to me. I was horrified. I was absolutely riddled with guilt. I knew I had killed her but I dared not mention it to anyone. I was in a frightful state. With every day that passed, I grew more introverted and worried.

I started to go on long walks all by myself, a thing I had never done before. I used to walk and walk. Then, one day, I had the feeling that I wasn't alone. I knew that Daisy was beside me.

Suddenly, I saw her standing immediately in front of me. She was staring right through me with a terribly knowing expression in her eyes. It was as if I could hear her saying, 'You did it. You did it.'

I started to run. I had to get away. But Daisy was still beside me. I knew she was going to haunt me for ever.

It took me months to outgrow this terrifying experience. It convinced me that Auntie Frances had passed on to me some sort of supernatural power. I still believe I have it. I honestly believe that it is possible for me to cook someone's goose if they do something unpleasant to me.

I had to go through a great climactic thing facing up to this frightening power. I knew if I was to have any peace at all I had to decide once and for all just what my code of behaviour was going to be. I am now terribly careful even in my thoughts so far as people I dislike are concerned.

The man I was in love with went through all the motions of appearing suitably heartbroken at Daisy's death but this didn't stop him seeing me. Of course he never knew how I had felt about Daisy. He used to come to my home and my parents encouraged him like mad. They thought he was old enough to have a steadying influence on me. It was still an exciting relationship because we had so many interests in common. He was a designer and he used to take me to shows and exhibitions and we would argue furiously. But, after Daisy's death, it was not much good. I had a guilty conscience I couldn't control. And, in any case, it was just about this time that I met Alexander. After that, there was very little time to go to the local tennis club or to do any of the things I had enjoyed previously. A whole new world opened up.

There was never a day when Alexander failed to produce some dotty idea of how we should spend our time. I think he spent his time in bed in the daytime cooking up crazy ways of trying out something new.

We had one great game to fall back on when we had nothing better to do. We used to travel from Goldsmiths' to Charing Cross by train every evening with a friend of ours – also a great eccentric – John Wood, who had been at school with Alexander.

One of us, usually Alexander, because he is able to keep still for a long time apparently without breathing, would get into the luggage rack and pretend to be dead. John and I used to sit in opposite corners of the compartment looking very overcome and morose and we would wait until someone got in at one of the intermediate stations. Then, when the train started off with its usual jerk, Alexander would suddenly go bump and roll over and the strangers in the compartment would jump up and look round frantically for a way of escape, absolutely terrified.

Or we would pretend to be religious maniacs and walk round Trafalgar Square going up to people and asking them if they knew about the Coming of the Lord and things like that. It is extraordinary the reactions one gets.

Then there was the bath chair stunt. That never failed to create a sensation. Alexander used to meet me at Charing Cross station with a bath chair that belonged to his mother. He would lift me out of the compartment very gently and put me into it. Everyone would stand aside and we would hear them saying, 'Poor thing. And so young! What a tragedy!'

Then, suddenly, when we had swept through the barrier like V.I.P.s, I would leap out of the chair and everyone around would be simply furious.

Very occasionally, on the day that Alexander's allowance came in, he would decide we would be grand. We would go to Quaglino's ... Alexander still wearing his prune pants and his mother's pyjama top as a shirt and me in a gingham skirt, very short, a black poplin shirt, knee socks and sandals. Our appearance must have been sensational and I can only think the waiters regarded us as the children of eccentric millionaires. We always had the best champagne and Alexander always paid by cheque in enormous style.

One night when we were going to Quaglino's, Alexander turned up at Charing Cross station in evening dress ... or, rather, his version of evening dress. He had managed to get hold of some evening trousers and a jacket and he had borrowed a collar from someone and made a reasonably good-looking bow tie out of the belt of one of his mother's old macintoshes. The trouble was that he hadn't been able to get hold of a shirt so he had just painted buttons the right distance apart down his chest. It was quite effective at a distance but a ghastly shock when you came close to.

I felt terribly shy and nervous when we walked into Quaglino's. I thought Alexander looked rather splendid but I was wearing a home-made grey flannel tunic well above my knees and mustard stockings. Even to me this seemed completely inappropriate. However Alexander was in complete charge of the situation as usual and we had a marvellous evening.

All this may sound a bit silly now but we were both about sixteen at the time. After a night out like this Alexander had very little money to live on until the next cheque came in. He worked it out that he could live on four shillings a day. He had one meal a day at four o'clock in the afternoon when he got out of bed. It was always the same … spaghetti and a meat loaf. When I was with him, we shared it.

The spaghetti was salted and boiled, then dumped on a plate. Then Alexander would open a tin of meat loaf and shake it out on top of the spaghetti. The fat round the meat loaf sort of melted into the hot spaghetti. It looked revolting but it seemed very chic and international to us.

Every minute I was free from Goldsmiths' I spent with Alexander. His mother was still in the country and far too ill to come back to Chelsea. The squalor in the house with Alexander living there alone was incredible. He started off sleeping in his own bedroom. After about a month or so of this, the bed seemed a bit grubby even to him and he was bored with all the dirty glasses round the floor, the ghastly stubbed-out cigarettes and the empty bottles. He moved to his mother's room and when, after a few months, this was in pretty much the same state as his own room, he moved on to the spare room, then to the servant's room. It was too sordid for words. He never washed up anything so the kitchen was awful. He used every plate, every piece of cutlery in the house and these just remained stacked up by the sink week after week. He used to take the top plate and the handiest knife and fork out of the pile by the sink and just wash these when he needed them. To me, this way of life was distinctly cosmopolitan and exciting. It was the right background for our first experiments in sex.

Alexander had no use for straightforward sex at all. Intellectual sex was the thing. What this meant was that we read extremely advanced books on the subject and tried to keep up with them. We were heavily experimenting but both of us were, in fact, terribly innocent. We just thought of ourselves as 'advanced'. We know now that it was all rather pathetic. And the ending was always the same ... spaghetti and meat loaf!

I had been brought up strictly. The importance of virginity had been drilled into me and I was really extremely frightened of sex. I had had lots and lots of boy friends from an early age because I was at co-educational schools and have always liked boys better than birds. Generally I get along with them far more easily. But the experimenting with Alexander was something quite new to me.

I suppose it really was rather funny: Alexander presenting himself as a much older and more experienced person than he really was ... so experienced, in fact, that he had come to the conclusion that very advanced sex was the only thing worth having ... and me, absolutely terrified of losing my virginity.

All my poor parents had succeeded in instilling into me was the fact that so long as I didn't do the normal thing, it was all right. I believed everything Alexander said and I convinced myself quite easily that if I didn't do the one thing which I had been told was unforgivable, this was simply an exciting essential of education.

It was quite different for Alexander: he had none of my doubts and fears. He had generations of advanced thinkers behind him. He was – I know now – trying, in his own way, to live up to his image of his father, a man who was pretty fantastic-looking and bound to capture the imagination of any small boy.

Richard Plunket Greene, Alexander's father, has been described by his Oxford friend, Evelyn Waugh, as 'piratical in appearance, sometimes wearing ear-rings, a good man with a boat, a heavy smoker of dark, strong tobacco'.

He and Alexander's mother, Elizabeth Russell, were divorced when Alexander was eight years old so that his memories of his father, during his most impressionable years, were of an exciting stranger, a tall, handsome, buccaneering man in naval uniform who turned up out of the blue at rare intervals with exciting stories of the war and the navy.

To Alexander, then about ten or eleven, and living in the strongly feminine atmosphere of his grandmother's house at Shere in the company of the sixteen girl evacuees aged from three to thirteen who had been billeted on her, the rare occasions when he saw his father were enough to inspire something very like hero-worship.

During the war years when I had been going from school to school, in various places in Kent and later in Wales, Alexander was living with his grandmother, his only companions, apart from the evacuees in the house, his cousins, the Blakiston girls, whose father is a big noise at the Public Records Office and who were living at nearby Clandon Park where the Royal Archives were housed for the duration of the war.

All Alexander's relations and ancestors have been big noises of one sort or another. He is immensely proud of the fact that Bertrand Russell is a cousin and that his name appeared prominently on Hitler's black list of those to be exterminated at the earliest possible moment. On the other hand, when we were invited to lunch at Woburn with Caterine Milinaire, he didn't even mention that he happened to be a member of the family. He thinks he has inherited much of what he calls his 'decadence' from his father's side of the family. His grandmother, Gwen Plunket Greene, was the daughter of Sir Hubert Parry and the favourite niece of the theologian, von Hügel. She grew up amongst the late Victorian musical and artistic surroundings of 'The Souls' and had rather an awful childhood, always overshadowed by a brilliant sister.

Perhaps because of this, she completely ruined her own children. She thought them perfect and kept telling them so. They had no correction, direction or discipline. In her eyes, they could do no wrong. She treated them as equals. There was no division between the generations as there is in most families.

'Look at the results,' Alexander says. 'My father has never achieved anything much in spite of all the advantages and natural gifts he had. Amongst other things, he might have been a good musician; he studied the organ with Albert Schweitzer at one time; instead, he probably made my mother miserable and he has never given me much of the help a son is normally given by his father. Uncle David took to drugs and was finally found drowned in a lake near my grandmother's cottage at Longleat; and Aunt Olivia, though she did achieve the somewhat doubtful privilege of being Paul Robeson's girl friend at a time when he was much in demand and was famous for stunning people at grand dinner parties with remarks like "I love the sound of flesh on flesh", was hopelessly neurotic and miserable although great fun.' Because of this family history, to spoil children in childhood and adolescence is, to Alexander, the worst thing any parent can do.

I certainly had none of this.

One day when we were on our way to the Chelsea house, Alexander told me he had a surprise for me. I wouldn't recognize the place. The floors had been swept, the dishes washed up and there were clean sheets on the beds. Apparently an aunt of his had got wind of the awful state of the house and she had suggested to his mother that she simply must get some household services to come in and clean up. This was arranged and Alexander was told to expect a woman to call and do the cleaning.

When the door bell rang one morning soon afterwards, he opened the door, expecting to find some cosy old Mrs Mop on the doorstep. Instead, there was a frightfully pretty girl. She was just as surprised as he was. She thought she had come to the wrong house, having been told some woman with rheumatism needed help. She had just left school and was filling in time with odd holiday jobs until she went up to university.

Alexander went on to tell me the story of this meeting with enormous relish. Both he and the girl were rather shy at first and while she bustled round with brooms and dustpans and things, he just stood around getting in the way. He was a bit embarrassed about the whole thing … this pretty girl seeing the mess he had made of the house.

Finally he said, 'I think I ought to take you out to lunch.'

And she said, 'That would be nice.'

So they went to lunch and afterwards he said, 'I think you've done enough; I ought to take you to the movies.'

And she said, 'That would be nice.'

So they went to the movies.

Afterwards she was struck by conscience and they went back to the house and made up beds together and swept up some more of the dust.

And Alexander said, 'I think I ought to take you out to dinner.'

And she said, 'That would be nice.'

But, in fact, when he checked, he found he hadn't any money left. So they had spaghetti and meat loaf.

And then she seduced him which was absolutely marvellous. The next day she was off to Cambridge and he never saw her again.

That's the way Alexander told the story. I was insanely jealous … he meant me to be. It forced me to make a decision I had been trying to make for a long time. I simply had to leave home. As a result of the life I was leading, my relationship with my parents was appalling. But I had absolutely no money and simply couldn't afford to live anywhere else. I had failed to get the Art Teachers' Diploma at Goldsmiths'. I knew I had to find a job. In spite of the never-ending rows at home, I was determined I was not going to be a teacher.

Finally, after searching round and making endless inquiries, I got a job in the workroom of Erik, the milliner, in Brook Street. I was paid £2. 10s. 0d. a week. Out of this I had to pay my fares from Blackheath and buy stockings and that sort of thing. There was never any money for food and I spent nothing on clothes. I made all these myself, sitting up most of the night to remake the same dresses year after year and try to give them something of a new look. Alexander had left Goldsmiths' too. He had a sort of job as a photographer in the King's Road.

These were tough times for us. We were both terribly pushed for money but we were still living this extraordinary life of either going to Quaglino's or somewhere grand like that and having everything we wanted to eat or being actually starving.

I was supposed to stop work at five o'clock in the evening but, in fact, I was nearly always there until seven. It wasn't Erik's fault. It was just that I used to get so excited and engrossed in something I was making that I simply couldn't stop. Alexander used to come to Brook Street to meet me.

We were still at the stage of showing off to each other. Alexander would take me to a bar for a drink and I would order a Scotch because I thought this was the advanced thing to do. I would never tell him that I had had nothing to eat all day so he wasn't prepared for the fact that as soon as I had downed the Scotch, I would faint.

As soon as Alexander realized what was causing these fainting attacks, he took to arriving at Brook Street with a wing of chicken or something like that in a bit of greaseproof paper and he would make me eat this instantly standing in the street if necessary before we did anything else.

I could have been fed perfectly well at home; the trouble was that I never got home until all the rest of the family were in bed and as I had to catch a train soon after seven o'clock in the morning, I was never up in time to have any breakfast.

The only time I had anything to eat before Alexander arrived to collect me in the evenings were those days when the rather charming Jamaicans working in the kitchens of Claridge's, next door to the workrooms, would bang on our door and say; 'Hey, do you want some breakfast?' This would happen on mornings when there happened to be lots of left-overs ... kidneys and things like that ... from room service upstairs. And when there was a wedding reception or a big party in the hotel, these Jamaicans would bring in to us those delicious but rather ghastly-looking remains. They tasted pretty good when you had had nothing else to eat all day. There were, too, the isolated days when Erik's new collection went over particularly well with the Press and then he would buy us all a tremendous lobster lunch to celebrate.

But it was terribly up and down. I was either eating things like caviare and lobster or else nothing at all. And the days when there was nothing at all were much the most frequent.

It may have been as a result of this, I don't know. It may have been to appease his mother who really was wonderful and incredibly understanding but who did say, occasionally, 'Really, Alexander, I think you ought to have a go at something soon.' Suddenly, Alexander was overcome by embarrassment at leading what was virtually a non-working life. He was pretending to be a photographer but he really had very little interest and he took so little trouble that nobody was taken in.

He went off and got himself a job at Selfridge's. He was wildly enthusiastic at first and full of fantasies about ending up a buyer for the Lewis Group who had just taken over the store. But it wasn't really his kind of life at all.

He earned about seven pounds a week and on pay nights we would usually go to a party and then on to the Embassy Club for breakfast with a great friend of ours, Lindsay Masters. We would have a terrific time. Lindsay and Alexander nearly always joined the band in the jazz numbers. At the end he would find his seven pounds just about enough to cover our bill.

It was all rather ridiculous. It soon became obvious that a career at Selfridge's wasn't going to work out. The only extra money he was earning was when he played his trumpet at deb parties. He was usually paid for this in advance and we would go out and blow it all on drink before the party so that Alexander wouldn't be exactly in the mood. So this didn't last long either!

By this time we had a lot of friends amongst the Fulham Road crowd. And Alexander had been given his first secondhand car – a Morris Minor. Our most pressing problem was still the same … we never had any money. We had time on our hands but no money to help us pass it pleasantly. We simply had to invent things that would be exciting to do and would not involve dough.

We both still dressed in rather an extraordinary way, particularly Alexander. But my dresses were odd, too. I was beginning to get more daring in the invention of my own clothes. People used to look at us wherever we went. They would laugh at us and sometimes shout after us, 'God, this Modern Youth!'

We decided we would use this to our own advantage and get our own back. We started to call ourselves 'Modern Youth'. When we met, one of us would say, 'Shall we be Modern Youth tonight?' And we would set up some wicked nonsense.

Sometimes we gave concerts in the streets. We would go to Covent Garden and Alexander and his jazz friends would play and we would all dance together in the streets. The men working on the fruit and vegetables and flowers loved it and they would often join in. Finally we had lots of regular companions on these jaunts. Some of them had cars and we got ourselves pretty well organized.

One night we went down to Harrow and gave a concert outside the school. Some of the boys came out in their pyjamas to join in and we heard afterwards they had been expelled. We gave up the concerts after that but, while they lasted, they were wild fun.

We took to police baiting instead. The police are splendid material for anything like this because they take things so seriously. You have only got to scamper across a road at night with a parcel under your arm and drive off quickly and they will follow you all the way to Richmond.

One rather miserable day when we hadn't anything much to do we decided it would be fun to find out just how ordinary people in the street would react to kidnapping. We chose South Kensington tube station because we knew there were bound to be lots of people about.

There were four of us that day; a young sculptor friend who in the football jersey he wore looked more like a thug than an artist; a very extraordinary girl friend – a long, thin girl who looked marvellously convincing when we had dressed her up in a ghoulish way, Alexander and me. Alexander's hair was very long and he soaked it with vaseline, scraped it back and put a little lipstick round his eyes. This had the most extraordinarily sinister effect. I was supposed to look like a nice, ordinary, respectable girl.

The idea was that I should walk along outside the station with the ghoulish girl following a few steps behind me. Alexander was to drive up with this thuggish-looking type beside him and as I came alongside the car, he was to stop, throw open the door and the 'thug' would make a grab at me. At the same moment the girl walking behind me would close up quickly and give me a push into the car.

It all worked pretty well according to plan until the last minute. The car stopped, the door was flung open, the thug grabbed me and the girl behind started pushing. I made all the right noises. The trouble was that because it was raining, I was carrying an umbrella and it happened to be rather a cherished possession. It got stuck in the door. I had to be pushed out before I could get it shut.

The reaction in the street was extraordinary. In seconds, it seemed to us, a taxi had stopped across our bows blocking the way. There were people hanging on to the car and shouting for the police. There seemed to us to be hundreds of them. They were shaking their fists at us – I must say we must have looked pretty sinister – and we were clinging to the door handles inside the car to prevent them getting at us and lynching us. One man, rather dramatically, stood in front of the car with his arms outstretched shouting, 'If you drive off now, you will kill me and it will be murder. Murder is a lot worse than kidnapping!'

All the noise and the shouting and the angry faces peering into the car were absolutely terrifying. I burst into genuine tears. Suddenly, somehow, the thing had gone too far.

I don't know what would have happened if the sound of police bells from all directions hadn't diverted the attention of the crowd for a moment. I suppose they relaxed because they felt the police had arrived to take over. Alexander took a chance, put his foot down hard on the accelerator and managed to swerve right out across the road. We went roaring round South Kensington station and as we rushed up the Fulham Road, it seemed to us that the whole of the Metropolitan Police were after us. Fortunately we knew the district rather well and Alexander drove straight for a rather decrepit, deserted mews. We jumped out of the car, scrubbed the make-up off our faces with handkerchiefs, covered the car with leaves and sacks and bits of rubbish that had been left lying around and left it there. We dashed into the nearest cinema and saw the programme round twice before we dared come out. It was a couple of days before we collected the car.

Then we had one of our lucky breaks. Alexander was looking through a drawer at home when he found a pair of cufflinks he had forgotten all about. They had been left to him by his Uncle David ... the elegant David Plunket Greene, described by Waugh as 'a languid dandy devoted to all that was fashionable'.

Uncle David's idea of what was fashionable was not Alexander's. He thought the cufflinks were ghastly things but, hoping he might be able to raise a bit of money on them, he took them to a pawn-broker in the King's Road who offered him forty pounds. This made him suspect that they might be worth a great deal more so he took them to a firm in Bond Street. They gave him three hundred and fifty pounds. This was an incredible amount of money to us. Alexander paid off all our debts, bought a tape recorder he had been coveting for ages and decided that as we would probably never again have so much ready cash, the thing to do was for us to go on holiday. We went to the South of France and started living rather grandly. When we discovered the money wasn't going to last long that way, we moved along the coast to less known, less expensive, places and we stayed in the sun till all the money was spent.

We came back to Chelsea penniless again but bursting with good health and ready for anything.

We started spending a lot of our time at Finch's. Here we met all sorts of widely different people ... very clever young architects, painters, musicians, sculptors, film directors and layabouts congregated there. They were all pretty interesting. There was a great deal of drinking, mostly whisky unfortunately, which we really couldn't afford. Anyway, I don't like whisky so I used to spend most of my time faking.

It was here that we first met Archie McNair through a great friend of ours, Michael Wallis, who was working with him. Archie had a photography business in the King's Road. Our first reaction to him was not too good. In the first place, he wore a suit and carried an umbrella and brief case. He was an ex-solicitor who had fallen in love with Chelsea life but still retained the rather precise and pedantic way of expressing himself that one associates with lawyers. He seemed oddly out of place in his own photographic studios and this in itself was odd as it was there that the whole Chelsea revolution was conceived. It was odd, too, because it was he who rationalized the mood in the air. The coffee bars, the restaurants and even Bazaar would not have happened if he had not spotted the talent of the people who sat around in his studio drinking his coffee. Nor would they have happened without his flair for property and his knowledge of the law and business.

When we first met him, he was just about to open a coffee bar in the King's Road ... the second coffee bar in London I think ... and he invited Alexander to go in with him as his partner. At that time Alexander and I both thought of coffee bars as a shortlived flash in the pan ... a craze that would be over and done with in six months' time ... and Alexander refused. Many times we regretted this. Archie's coffee bar was called the Fantasy and immediately after the opening was well known and crowded every night. It became the centre of the social life of Chelsea ... the whole Chelsea thing really brewed up there ... between the Fantasy, Finch's and Archie's studio. Nobody has ever been able to make up his mind precisely what 'the Chelsea Set' was but I think it grew out of something in the air which developed into a serious effort to break away from the Establishment. It was the first real indication of a complete change of outlook. The fact that this change gathered momentum so much more quickly than anyone ever imagined was unpredictable.

The unwitting originators of this renaissance were the core and inspiration of a revival of the creative arts. All of them have since achieved something in their own particular field. They were the first genuine break-away group. They are all exciting. Ultimately their ideas had enormous influence on people everywhere and on their way of thinking. They were far more important than those who eventually hit the headlines and were called 'the Chelsea Set' in the Press and eventually produced a feeling that the whole thing was rather bogus. At any rate, we did not see ourselves as being a part of any particular 'set'. We spent our time in Chelsea and the people we knew all had different things to recommend them. Our friends and acquaintances were painters, photographers, architects, writers, socialites, actors, con-men, and superior tarts. There were racing drivers, gamblers, T.V. producers and advertising men. But somehow everyone in Chelsea was that much more positive and go-ahead and, if not the greatest in their field, at least the most passionately involved.

I became quite caught up in the excitement of the King's Road and I knew that it was the only place I really wanted to live. The opportunity came when Alexander and Archie together decided it would be fun for the three of us to work together. We had endless discussions and eventually it was agreed that if we could find the right premises for a boutique in the King's Road, we would open a shop. It was to be a *bouillabaisse* of clothes and accessories ... sweaters, scarves, shifts, hats, jewellery and peculiar odds and ends. We would call it Bazaar. I was to be the buyer. Alexander inherited £5,000 on his twenty-first birthday and Archie was prepared to put up £5,000 too.

This was something I desperately wanted to do. But I was terribly worried. I felt the enormous responsibility of having Archie and Alexander risk their all on me. I wondered whether I had perhaps over-persuaded them. I was also a little scared about giving up the weekly (though tiny) pay packet of a regular job. On the other hand, Alexander and I had already decided that we were not going to lead separate working lives. We had already determined that somehow we would find a way of earning our living together.

Then we had another bit of luck. We were in the Markham Arms with Archie when we heard that the solicitors who then occupied the ground floor and basement of Markham House next door were moving out. Alexander had been in love with this house for ages, its great attraction to him being the basement which he wanted to turn into a cool jazz night club, but we had never thought there would be any chance of us getting it as the two upper floors were occupied by a statutory tenant and we imagined the lawyers would be there for ever.

Even when we were told that night that the law firm were moving out we didn't really think we would ever be able to aspire to such premises but Alexander and Archie decided they would find out what the possibilities were and eventually, after a lot of difficulties, borrowing money and raising a mortgage and all that sort of thing, we were able to buy the freehold. We got it for £8,000.

We knew the alterations we would have to make at Markham House would take six months at least but Alexander and Archie said that I would need at least as much time as this to go round and make myself known to the wholesalers and buy stock for the opening. They agreed to pay me five pounds a week during this time. I left Erik's.

Archie found a bedsitting-room to let in Oakley Street at a price I could afford. Tony was the one who had to break the news to my parents. Fortunately Tony supported us all the way. Somehow he managed to fix it for me at home but not without still more appalling family scenes.

Our plans for Markham House got under way. We were going to have a really good jazz club ... very comfortable, very chic ... in the basement. The boutique was to be on the ground floor. We decided we would have to strip out the front of the house to take a wide shop window and remove the old iron railings that cut us off from passers-by. Then, if we filled in the old gaping area, we would have a very useful forecourt.

We asked an architect friend – still a student – to plan these alterations for us. He made an extremely good job of it but unfortunately overlooked the fact that Town Planning permission is essential if any sort of structural alteration is being done. There was a very nasty moment when, having removed the front of the house and put in the shop window, we were ordered to restore the building to its original state.

There was only one thing for us to do. We had to see the London County Council architects and somehow persuade them that we were doing the right thing. We went along to their offices ... Alexander, Archie, the architect and I. When our names were announced we were told that it was quite impossible for us to have a personal interview. We all sat down. Archie said that our business was so serious that we would simply have to wait there until someone could find time to see us. We sat in absolute silence. To me it seemed like hours. I was convinced we were ruined. We were bankrupt. We could never hope to rise above this. It was all so ghastly and such an awful end to all we had planned and hoped for that when the Chief Architect finally came into the room, I was in tears. Maybe it was this that made him relent a little. Anyway, he said he would inspect the building the next day and decide then what had to be done.

Fortunately when a proper survey was made it was discovered that if some rebuilding was not done – and done quickly – the whole place might fall down. It had no proper foundations and the marshy ground on which it is built had subsided over the years. It was agreed that provided we were willing to put in proper foundations and make the whole building structurally sound to the surveyor's specifications, we would be given permission to carry on. We were so thankful that we accepted without thinking of the cost. In fact it turned out to be a frightfully expensive business pumping in all the concrete necessary to strengthen the foundations.

We were just beginning to get over this setback when we discovered we had offended the Chelsea Society. We began getting abusive and anonymous letters accusing us of vandalism and all sorts of other nasty things. People used to come and stand on the pavement outside Markham House and shake their fists at us. The funny thing was that we hadn't done the thing they accused us of and kept shouting about. They said we had removed a beautiful bow window. There has never been a bow window in the part of the house we altered; it is on the other side of the façade and it is still there!

I think it was probably as a result of the awful publicity we got in the local Press inspired by members of the Chelsea Society that our application for a night club licence was turned down. Instead, we decided to do a new sort of restaurant in the basement. It was to be called Alexander's. We planned to open this and the boutique on the ground floor above simultaneously.

While the structural alterations and the decorations were going on, Alexander, Archie and I and the people involved with us in the work had to spend a lot of time at Markham House. We started going into the Markham Arms next door for a snorter of some sort at the end of the day. During these six months it became virtually the centre of such social life as we had time for.

At first we found it rather a horrible old pub ... a poor substitute for Finch's. It was usually empty when we went in with the exception of about half a dozen decayed regulars. As soon as we began to use it every day, and this became known, the whole thing changed. Old friends from Finch's started to turn up and they would bring their friends along and suddenly the whole thing snowballed. In about three weeks, in the way these things can happen, the Markham Arms became the busiest pub in the King's Road, even more crowded than Finch's. It was transformed from a dreary old meeting place for a few cronies into a terrific swinging club. It was constantly packed with people, all jostling to get in. Most of them ordered 'shorts'. It didn't take Mrs Andrews, the old woman who ran the Markham Arms, long to realize how profitable this was. She was getting a tremendous amount of publicity one way and another. She wanted to hang on to this extraordinary new state of things. When all the papers began to write about 'the Chelsea Set' and she heard people talking about it in the pub, she thought it was 'the Chelsea Six'. She was a bit deaf!

So far as she was concerned, the 'six' were us three and Jane Stewart, Kim Waterfield, Michael Alexander ... or whoever was in her favour at the time. She began to bombard Alexander and Archie and me with colossal presents. Every day one of us would be given something ... a case of champagne or six bottles of a Château-bottled claret or a magnum of cognac nailed up in a wooden crate.

About everything else she would be extraordinarly mean. One day Alexander ordered half a pint of bitter for me. Handing it across the bar rather carelessly, Mrs Andrews let it slip and poured it down my dress. I kept saying to her, 'Quick! Quick! Please give me a sponge or something.' Instead, she screamed at the top of her voice so that everyone in the pub could hear, 'Don't worry. Don't worry. I'll make it up to you.'

To quieten me down, Alexander whispered to me, 'Forget it. She'll give you a new dress.' But she didn't. She gave me another half pint of bitter!

We had to keep on going into the Markham Arms because we knew that if we did not succeed in our application for a wine licence for Alexander's, we'd be forced to rely on her for wines for the restaurant.

The amazing thing was that she went on giving us all these terrific presents until we did manage to get a licence of our own. That day, the moment the news got around, they stopped dead.

When I wasn't at Markham House supervising the rebuilding and redecorating that was going on, I was dashing round the wholesalers with Alexander or going round the art schools to meet the students and see their work. Art schools are treasure haunts of original design. I was able to buy all the jewellery I wanted for the opening of Bazaar this way.

Any spare time I had I used to make hats. Alexander used to take these to stores like Peter Jones and he managed to sell quite a few at about eight or nine guineas each. We also managed to sell some to rich girl friends. It all helped!

We still dressed in an extraordinary way and obviously we did not impress average business people. When we went into a wholesaler's showrooms and said we had come to see what they had so that we might buy for a boutique we were opening in the King's Road, people just didn't believe us. It proved almost impossible to get anyone to give us any attention at all. They thought we were student nut cases; they ignored us when they weren't being downright unpleasant. There were times when they were incredibly rude.

Fortunately for our morale there were exceptions. Harold Rose of Dorville was sweet to us. He could not have been more understanding and helpful. He really backed us like mad. He was even willing to make things specially for us. He gave us a little of the confidence we so badly needed after the experiences we had with other members of the fashion trade who were frankly beastly.

Of course I realize that the way we started was quite crazy. Everything we ordered had to be delivered to Alexander's mother's house in Chelsea while the shop was being built. This was the only place there was room to stock it. We used to spread everything we bought out on the floor. We would spend hours walking round looking at it all, wondering if we should ever sell it and having no idea at all what we should charge.

Alexander made inquiries and discovered that the normal gross profit was 33⅓%. What we didn't realize was that to get a return of 33⅓% you have to put 50% on cost. By marking up our stuff one-third we were actually only getting something like 25% and underselling every other shop in London. As a result, when we did open, we were gunned at by all the local tradespeople. Obviously they complained to the wholesalers who promptly telephoned us.

'You can't buy from us any more,' they said. 'You are underselling our fixed retail prices.'

It was no wonder we did such a roaring trade the moment we opened. We found out – too late – that on some things we were actually losing money. We had estimated that we might – with luck – expect to take about a hundred pounds a week. During the first week we took five hundred. It was terrifying. We were always selling out of things that were going well simply because we had no idea how much stock we ought to carry. The shop was constantly stripped bare – sometimes we hardly had enough to dress the window – because we never bought enough of anything.

It was unbelievable to us that there should be so many people wanting to buy the sort of things we had to sell. I don't know how we survived the awful hand-to-mouth existence of those first weeks. But they did prove that there was a real need for fashion accessories for young people chosen by people of their own age. The young were tired of wearing essentially the same as their mothers.

Alexander's opened to the public a few weeks before Bazaar was ready. Archie knew so much about catering by this time through his experience with the Fantasy that all the final plans for the restaurant went through comparatively easily. And, fortunately, it went well from the start.

Encouraged by this, we decided to give a party for the opening of Bazaar. We wanted to ask the Press but we didn't know any of them and they knew nothing of us. We went through the papers and magazines together, picked out a few likely sounding names and sent invitations. Our whole approach was so unprofessional that it is not surprising none of them turned up. Some of them sent junior assistants. But the excitement in the King's Road was tremendous.

We put up a marquee in the forecourt outside Markham House, a tremendously bright, striped affair with side panels about six feet high so that passers-by couldn't actually see in without standing on tip-toe or balancing on the top of upturned shopping baskets. We had a long trestle table loaded with nosh and booze and a burning brazier in one corner to give a cosy, welcoming atmosphere. Some of the waiters from Alexander's down below came up to help.

All our old friends from Finch's and the Markham Arms turned up and it was a terrific party. There were lots of would-be gate crashers and people outside queued to give each other a lift to see what was going on in the marquee.

The party went z-o-o-m from the start. So did Bazaar. People literally rushed in. And they gathered in the forecourt, sometimes six deep at a time, either liking it tremendously – or hating it.

In ten days, we hadn't a single piece of the original merchandise in the place.

Apart from hats, I designed only one original thing for the opening ... a pair of mad house-pyjamas. These were snapped up by *Harper's Bazaar* who gave us our first fashion editorial. The only other recognition we got from the Press was two or three paragraphs in the social columns ... rather awful paragraphs headed something like 'Alexander Plunket Greene, kinsman of the Duke of Bedford, opens shop in Chelsea'.

The trade ignored us. They laughed at us openly. They called us degenerate. They raised their eyebrows in mystified amazement. Later, when they realized how successful Bazaar was proving, they called our success a 'flash in the pan'. It was utterly impossible for them – or for us – to envisage that within seven years the business would go well over the million mark and the clothes I was to design would be in 150 shops in Britain, 320 stores throughout America and also on sale in France, Italy, Switzerland, Kenya, South Africa, Australia, Canada and, in fact, in just about every country in the western world.

A few days after *Harper's* returned the pyjamas to us after photographing them for the magazine, an American manufacturer came into the shop and bought them. As he was paying the bill, he said casually that he was taking them back to the States as he thought they would go rather well over there and he planned to put the design into mass production. I was furious but I couldn't say anything. It seemed terrible to me that he should buy a design of mine with the declared intention of copying. I ought to have been frightfully excited and flattered that any manufacturer could see a mass market potential in the one garment I had designed.

Perhaps, subconsciously, it was this that inspired me to concentrate seriously on designing. I had always wanted the young to have fashion of their own ... absolutely twentieth-century fashion ... but I knew nothing about the fashion business. I didn't think of myself as a designer. I just knew that I wanted to concentrate on finding the right clothes for the young to wear and the right accessories to go with them. At this stage, Alexander and Archie and I thought of Bazaar solely as a retail operation.

The trouble was that when it came to stocking the shop and keeping it stocked, I couldn't find the things I wanted. I decided that I would have to try and make these things myself. I bought Butterick paper patterns and cut out pieces where I didn't want them and added more paper where I did. I also started going to a few frantic evening classes on cutting. I bought the materials at Harrods as no one had told me about buying cloth wholesale.

I also bought a sewing machine. And I found a dressmaker who was willing to come in for a few hours a day and work for me. It wasn't long before she was working for me full time. Then I found another ... and another. My bedsitting-room was full of sewing machines and there were pieces of cloth all over the place. I had to move lengths of cloth and paper patterns from my bed before I could get into it at night. To add to the confusion I had two Siamese cats at the time. They used to eat the paper patterns. It took me some time to discover that the tissue paper used to make these patterns is manufactured from some by-product of fish bones!

It was an extremely crude way of working. If we had not succeeded in producing garments that sold at once, it would have been disastrous. I had to sell one day's output before I had the money to go out and buy more material. Luckily it soon became known that six o'clock was the best time to get the new dresses. The day's output from Oakley Street reached Bazaar about then and the dresses would be sold that evening so I'd be able to dash along to Harrods again in the morning with more money to spend.

I don't think that bedsitter of mine will ever recover from its spell as a factory. It was really rather a pretty room but the eccentric conditions under which we were working made it look appalling. And because I was buying my cloth over the counter at Harrods, there wasn't a great deal of profit.

Profits were kept low, too, by our thoroughly amateur and peculiar way of doing business. At first customers terrified us. We used to keep a bottle of Scotch under the counter and although I have never liked it, I found it gave me the courage I needed to deal with the more frightening ones. Often they turned out to be charming people; we grew to like them and then we would offer them a drink too and this set up a completely new way of selling because in a short time a great many of our customers were also friends and Bazaar became a sort of permanently running cocktail party.

People would tell us that when they had nothing special to do, they would say, 'Let's drop in and see what's going on at Bazaar', or 'Let's see what Plunket's up to now?' (Alexander was still called Plunket then). The whole thing was bedlam – a complete gamble. What with drinks and having food sent up for our friends from the restaurant at night, Archie discovered we spent £3,000 on entertaining alone in the first year. The marvellous thing about having a restaurant below was that we could entertain our friends far more lavishly than we can now.

The consolation for having spent all this money was that we knew we were on to a good thing. I moved from the bedsitter in Oakley Street to a flat over the Fantasy in the King's Road. We hired a cutter.

One day when we had hardly a dress left in the shop, I dashed along to the flat to collect one which I knew was being finished and, running back to Bazaar with the dress over my arm, I was stopped by a customer who grabbed the dress from me and said, 'That's the one I want; I'll have it.' She came into Bazaar with me and paid for it without trying it on.

We realized that we had to start thinking of expanding. Archie lent us the sitting-room of his house and this became an additional workroom.

We were so excited about the enormous success of the whole thing that we used to forget about shutting up the shop. We would stay open until we were absolutely out on our feet. Then we would go down to Alexander's for a nosh up. When we got there we would find the place crowded with people we knew so it was just a question of enough time to enable us to eat something and then we would open up Bazaar again and friends would come up with us and bring their friends and we would all have a brandy and they would still be with us at midnight or even in the early hours of the morning.

We were mad; the whole thing was hysterical. But people loved it. They loved coming up to the shop with husbands and boy friends late at night after a good dinner and looking through our things and trying on the dresses they liked and buying. It was because of all this that the shop developed such a marvellous character of its own. All sorts of exciting people used to come; interesting people who were really something. They would just strip off the dress they were wearing in the middle of the room and try on others.

Bazaar and Alexander's soon became a focal point of the King's Road, particularly on Saturday afternoons and in the evenings. Bazaar was undoubtedly helped by Alexander's because this was much more like a club than a restaurant. It was the second of the 'camp' restaurants in London. We call them 'camp' because of their theatrical atmosphere – very relaxed and casual – unlike the dear old Savoy and restaurants of that kind.

Of course we could not have carried on in this way indefinitely and, in fact, it wasn't long before some 'informer' told the Shops Act inspectors.

Alexander and I were together working in Bazaar late one night when a man came in and told us we were being exploited by our bosses who had no right to make us work such long hours. He said he was going to report them and advised us to look for jobs elsewhere where we might find the management more considerate. He simply refused to believe that we were in charge and the shop belonged to us. He got rather bad-tempered about the whole thing. Finally, he said, 'It doesn't make any difference who you are; this sort of thing is not fair to other traders and the people employed by them.'

He was right … much as we hated to admit it at the time. We just had not thought of it in this way. After his visit, we stayed open late only on Saturday nights when we changed the window. This was the night when our old buddies from Finch's would drop in. They loved to have a hand in arranging the window and were always full of suggestions.

At the start I did the window myself with everything in it pinned absolutely flat on panels Alexander designed for me. I was very much under the influence of the American magazines and I admired the way *Esquire* did shirts and things – pinned flat. But these friends of ours were not content to let anything remain as it was for any length of time. They are all creative and experimental people and they produced some terrific ideas.

I very much wanted to get right away from the standard type of figure used in window dressing. These always seemed to stand with one toe pointed just a little ahead of the other looking very upstage and grand. I wanted figures with the contemporary high cheek-boned, angular faces and the most up-to-date hair cuts. I wanted them with long, lean legs, rather like Shrimpton's, and made to stand like real-life photographic models in gawky poses with legs wide apart, one knee bent almost at right angles and one toe pointing upwards from a heel stuck arrogantly into the ground. It was just at this time that photographic models were beginning to use the leaping about style.

I got one of our sculptor friends who happened to be working with a display firm to help me. The figures were colossally expensive because each one had to be made separately but they were sensational. The impact on passers-by was tremendous. We did some crazy things with these models. People did not always get the message we intended but, in fact, there was always some logical thinking behind everything we did. We wanted people to stop and look. We wanted to shock people. All the men and women who walk down the King's Road are not necessarily shoppers as they are in Oxford Street. Nobody goes to Oxford Street except to shop. The King's Road is different and we wanted Bazaar to become a sort of Chelsea Establishment. We wanted to entertain people as well as sell to them and four or five times a year we would put in a window which wasn't intended to sell anything ... there would be no clothes in it. It would be some colossal, extravant gesture meant as pure joke so that people passing by would say, 'Good heavens! Isn't Bazaar extraordinary!' And it would be worth while for them to cross the road simply to see what we were up to.

We wanted everyone to like the shop and to like what we were doing. We wanted to appeal to husbands and boy friends as well as to the birds. We purposely used masculine jokes and things we knew would appeal to men. We wanted them to say when walking down the King's Road to some restaurant or other, 'Let's walk past Bazaar and see what's happening!' We wanted the old ladies who had no intention of buying anything to stop and stare into the window and have some fun gossiping with their cronies about what a funny shop we were.

It didn't always work. Some of the passers-by admired the look of the window but, at first, the majority jeered. What they did not know was that Alexander and I were lurking behind a ventilation grille listening to every word they said. Sometimes it hurt but we soon learned that the more derisive the laughter at a new window display, the more things we were going to sell that week.

I always pretend I don't care what people say, but I do. I care dreadfully but this doesn't make me compromise much if I feel sure I'm right.

We had to be arrogant then. We had to make a sharp, shocking statement at the beginning to be noticed at all. Now that we are accepted, we don't have to shock any more. People say we do crazy things but we have never done anything just to be outrageous or because we wanted to do the opposite to what most people do; not on principle; and certainly never out of aggressiveness.

Dressing the window on Saturday night was something we really looked forward to. We had enormous fun. Once we used the model of a photographer strung up by his feet to the ceiling with the most enormous old-fashioned camera focused on a bird also suspended at the most incredible angle. We wanted to give the impression that here was a dress so outstanding that it was worth while getting into any position to have a good look at it. We wanted people to say, 'Why is this man upside down?' And we wanted them to feel that it was because the dress was so exciting. We wanted them to feel a little of the excitement we ourselves felt.

Another time we put the birds into country suits ... heavy tweeds and that sort of thing. One of them held a huge fishing rod – the kind a man might use when tunny fishing in the Pacific. It stretched right across the window. The end of the line dipped into an old-fashioned round goldfish bowl in which we had a real live goldfish swimming around.

I loved our holiday windows. One week we just filled the window with stacks and stacks of milk bottles and put a notice in front of them 'Gone Fishing'. The one bird in the window was just disappearing through the back in terrific holiday clothes. Another, we had all the figures in bathing suits made of Banlon stretch fabric with madly wide coloured stripes like rugger sweat shirts. Some had long sleeves. They were all strumming away on white musical instruments ... guitars and saxophones and trumpets ... the sort of things the pop players use. The models were sprayed completely white with bald heads and were wearing absolutely round goggle sun specs which had never been seen before then and were sensationally new.

We nearly had a disaster when we used a giant lobster. We had just one figure in the window, beautifully dressed and leading this lobster on a gold chain like a dog. We scrubbed the lobster out like mad before we put it in the window but the next morning the whole shop smelt ghastly and we were terribly worried that the stink might have got into the clothes.

We began to discover what an enormous influence on sales colour has. I found that it is possible to build a window to sell one colour and that on wet and depressing days people find bright colours irresistible. I began to experiment with the psychology of colour. I learned how to arrange colours so that one predominated and zoomed out to such an extent that I could guarantee this would be the colour people would buy. I suppose it is this sort of thing that is the secret of supermarket success.

Whenever I had any time at all on my hands I would experiment. I used to arrange piles of brightly coloured cotton squares in different shapes with one colour or another zooming out boldly from amongst a mass of others. I found eventually that the moment anyone walked into the shop, I could tell which colour they would pick out and buy.

I think it was because we were always experimenting that people began to realize we were trying really hard. It began to be accepted that when we had a sale, everything in it was absolutely genuine. We have never had anything specially made – or bought in anything – for a sale. We have simply relied on making the window as dramatic as possible. It has always been our policy to sell off everything at the end of each season absolutely regardless of whether we are making a profit or not. In fine weather we put all the clothes on rails outside the shop on the forecourt and have a 'barker' as in an old-time Victorian music hall.

At one time we hired beautiful girls to act as 'sandwich men'. These girls, elegantly dressed and looking tremendously chic, walked in the gutter along the King's Road and Brompton Road carrying the traditional type of sandwich boards with the announcement 'Come to Bazaar. MAD Reductions' printed in beautiful old playbill type. They were a sensation. People were staggered and couldn't resist the temptation to come along and find out what was going on.

We coined this tag line MAD REDUCTIONS and we found it a terrific success.

People became so interested in us that they tried to help. Many times we had telephone calls from complete strangers telling us of some marvellous penny-farthing bicycle or old Victorian pram they'd seen in some antique shop. I would rush out to go and see it. Quite often it would be lent for display without any charge at all. Even dealers began to phone us. If they got hold of a painted horse or some fun-fair things that they knew were likely to appeal to us, they'd let us know. All sorts of unexpected people helped us spontaneously and out of this grew the strangely personal character of Bazaar that has remained an essential part of the business.

One Christmas we decided we wanted the children to share in the fun and excitement we were having. We got a friend of ours – Anton Hille – who was a brilliant linguist, to dress up as Father Christmas. We hired an enormous street brazier and kept this blazing away on the forecourt all day. Father Christmas stood beside it ringing sleigh bells with a huge basket of brightly coloured lollipops at his side.

Anton was young and dashing and very witty … a terrific character. And he wore the most marvellous beard. He kept shouting out 'Merry Christmas' in all the different languages he knew.

Chelsea is very international. Children passing by and hearing 'Merry Christmas' called out to them in their own tongue were absolutely stunned. It seemed to them that Anton was their own special Father Christmas who had come all the way from home just to see them. Their parents and nannies were highly suspicious; they obviously thought they were about to be caught by some commercial thing, and at first they dragged the poor children away screaming at the tops of their voices.

Fortunately, the word soon got around that there was nothing commercial in it; it was simply the Christmas spirit and our celebration of the good things the year had brought us. All we wanted to do was to give a lollipop to the children and wish them a happy Christmas. In a day or two, everyone realized this. Suddenly the idea caught on. Anton was surrounded by children all day. He was tremendously social and chatted up the parents and nannies like mad. How they loved it! We gave away more than a hundred pounds' worth of lollipops that week. Anton was the best Father Christmas ever.

For a time he ran Alexander's restaurant for us. But he was really too attractive for a job like this. Husbands and boy friends never took to him. He had a passion for birds and whenever a man came in with a particularly attractive girl he would start talking ... recommending a wine and that sort of thing. After a while he would go up to their table and ask, 'How do you like the wine?' And because he was so charming, he was always asked to sit down and try some. At once, he'd start flirting madly with the girl and sometimes even succeed in carrying her off for the rest of the evening. Not to mention polishing off the wine for good measure!

Alexander's original intention had been to play jazz in the restaurant and I don't know why we didn't do this. We ended up by playing Bach ... the preludes and fugues mostly. Maybe it was a good thing for perhaps it softened the blow to Alexander's family when they heard he was not only running a restaurant but going into trade as well. The dress shop was, in fact, the harder for them to swallow ... the restaurant could be passed over lightly as an irresponsible little peccadillo which was all right.

Alexander has masses of relations ... mostly great-aunts. They live to an enormous age in his family. Many of them were blue stockings in their own generation and considered very go-ahead, dashing and dangerous in their day but the idea of any member of the family running a shop was highly shocking. They were prepared to put up with the Army or the Church or being a farmer (provided you made losses) or simply pottering about being a duke. But selling dresses was too much.

One of the family was sent to find out exactly what Alexander was up to. He wrote to Alexander's mother after having dinner in the restaurant and told her that the food was surprisingly good and that he enjoyed the music so much that he couldn't really remember very much else.

This inspired one of his great-aunts – Dolly Ponsonby – to visit the restaurant. Alexander says that she was, in fact, trying to be terribly good and understanding about the things we were doing and she thought she would be setting an example to other members of the family by supporting him. It wasn't that any of them were nasty; it was just that we were made to feel that what we were doing was not exactly what was expected of us.

When Dolly Ponsonby rang up to book a table, she asked the price of lunch. We were at that time running a special seven-and-sixpenny lunch as bait to bring in customers. The restaurant was always full in the evenings but in the middle of the day we were lucky if the place was fifty per cent full. We wanted it to look popular and gay to encourage business people to use Alexander's when entertaining clients and associates. The thing is that business entertaining is nearly always on a lavish scale what with cocktails before lunch, additional courses like smoked salmon and caviare, different wines with separate courses and liqueurs afterwards. The cost of a lunch like this would balance out the loss on the seven-and-sixpenny meals and we would break just about even.

We really gave a frightfully good lunch. At seven-and-six it was colossal value. I should think we lost about half-a-crown on each meal served at this price but it did achieve its purpose.

The waiter speaking on the telephone to Alexander's great-aunt Dolly told her that we had a set lunch at seven-and-sixpence but unfortunately she didn't get her facts right. She thought he said one-and-sixpence. She promptly booked a table, asked that Alexander should look after her personally and invited a cousin to join her.

When Alexander called in at the restaurant to see how things were going he found a very embarrassed cousin and some very embarrassed waiters. His cousin had looked at the menu and seen that the price was seven-and-six. But Dolly Ponsonby was still oblivious of the fact. She had glanced down the menu which gave an incredible choice of dishes for each course and had decided it was all far too much for any one person to eat. She had told the waiter that one lunch would be quite sufficient for the two of them. They would share this. They had half portions of every dish of the day and worked their way right through the menu.

Alexander tried to explain to the waiters. He told them she was a great-aunt and very old and they sort of touched their imaginary forelocks and said they understood. It turned out to be quite a test of their understanding. When the bill came, Great-aunt Dolly, without glancing at it, firmly put down one shilling and ninepence ... one-and-six for the lunch, threepence the tip. She thought it plenty.

Another great-aunt of Alexander's – Flora Russell – doubtless spurred on by Great-aunt Dolly's experience, decided to have a discreet look at the place before committing herself.

Alexander is devoted to Flora Russell who is now around ninety-seven years old and still the most incredibly energetic woman. She seems to know everyone in the whole world over sixty who is of any interest and she can tell fascinating stories about them all. She is the most amazing woman, interested in everything and everybody. She still wants to try everything new. When the Hovercraft first came into the news, she wrote to the inventor and said, 'I'm a very old lady and I would like to go on your Hovercraft.' And he wrote back and said, 'Do come.' And she loved it.

She still gets bored with any one place after any length of time and is quite ready to hop on a plane at a moment's notice and go to some other part of the world. So many of Alexander's family are in the Foreign Office that she has relatives of one kind or another all over the place and every now and then she will disappear on a sort of private Cook's tour round the world, staying at the various Embassies.

Through Flora Russell, Alexander has met the most amazing and splendid people. There were times when perhaps she might be staying at his home and his mother would say, 'What would you like to do this afternoon, Aunt Flora? We have got Trevelyan coming to dinner' – hoping, I suspect, that Flora might be willing to spend a quiet afternoon. Not a bit of it.

'Let's give Bertie a ring,' Flora would say. 'It would be nice to see him.'

And Alexander's mother, frightfully embarrassed, would have to telephone Bertrand Russell and say something like, 'I'm phoning for Flora and she would like you to come to tea.'

And Bertrand Russell would reply, 'Well, it is not very easy for me.' But he came. People always do, whoever they are, when Flora Russell wants to see them. Everyone always has done what Aunt Flora wants. Obviously she has been adored all her life. She must have been tremendous as a girl. She was one of the first women ever allowed to draw from the nude in mixed classes in a Paris art school. (It was considered quite all right for men to draw women in the nude but for women to do the same thing was indecent.)

She used to go on archaeological expeditions and on one of these near Florence she fell and broke her leg. I don't suppose it would have been in any way serious in these days but at that time doctors were not so clever at setting broken limbs and as a result she has been something of an invalid ever since. This does not deter her in anything she wants to do. She has got it all worked out.

Aunt Flo is undoubtedly an incredible old lady. She is still quite a good artist. She has drawn everybody who has been of interest in her generation … Sir Max Beerbohm … Sir William Orpen … anyone you can think of from the eighteen-nineties on. And she has a great collection of her own water colours which she longs to make into a book. This had become a sort of family joke. They are all terrified that she will go off one day and arrange for the publication of these and she will finance the whole thing herself and go broke.

Anyway, when Flora Russell decided to find out for herself just what Alexander was up to, she gave her driver instructions to go down the King's Road very slowly, particularly past Bazaar's window. As it happened, we had a tremendous hat in the window that day. It was a terrific hat. It had to be. It was priced at seventeen guineas.

When she got home, she wrote a note to Alexander: 'Dear Alexander,' it read, 'I drove past your shop and saw a hat in the window which was very charming and it was seventeen guineas. I – as you probably know – make hats. Shall I send you some?' Alexander replied at once. 'Dear Aunt Flo,' he wrote, 'your fortunes are made at last. You will be able to publish your book. Send me some hats and I'll flog them. With love, Alexander.'

Soon the hats arrived. Endlessly they arrived. Day after day there were hats and more hats. Followed by bills and invoices 'To one hat ... £16 10s. 0d.' At the bottom of each was a personal note, 'The rest is for you, my boy. You can keep it.'

The whole thing got completely out of hand. The hats were fantastic ... enormous things garlanded with masses of black tulle, tacked together with white thread because Aunt Flo is a bit short-sighted and mounted with birds and things poised at the most incredible angles. At first Alexander, looking ahead a bit, paid up. But that was nearly ten years ago!

We did not have to wait very long before the restaurant became known outside the confines of Chelsea. Several unexpected things helped. One day a man rang up and booked a table for four that evening. He arrived with his wife and with Prince Rainier and Princess Grace of Monaco. He took the head waiter aside immediately they walked in and said, 'I have a couple of rather distinguished guests with me this evening. I want you to know that if the newspapers are informed we will leave at once and, what's more, we will never come here again.'

The head waiter rang us up. Alexander said at once that there must be no mention under any circumstances of their presence.

We nipped round immediately he'd put the receiver down. They were sitting at Table One ... a table which is screened away from the others and normally used for business lunches or private parties. We got a table for ourselves opposite so that we could see everything that was going on without our interest being apparent. It was obvious that the Rainiers were mad about each other; they kept holding hands and touching each other under the table. And it was equally obvious that they were thankful to be in a place where they were ignored and left completely alone with their friends.

There were two detectives with them sitting at separate tables, each in one corner of the room. It was impossible not to know who they were. There were great bulges in their armpits ... obviously guns. We noticed that whilst the Rainiers and their friends were eating very simply – they had spaghetti – the detectives had terrific dinners ... caviare to begin with, crêpes suzette to end up with ... and the best French wines.

There was another very different evening ... when Brigitte Bardot came to dinner. This time a sort of mutter went round on the King's Road grapevine and immediately the restaurant was packed, absolutely swamped, with people.

Bardot preened herself like mad. The waiters, a particularly beautiful lot of young men, completely lost their heads and stopped serving people. They just stood around gaping. Bardot thought they were all terribly excited about her. If she had only known, they were far more excited by Jacques Charrier who was with her.

Then there was New Year's Eve ... our first New Year at Alexander's. It was quite awful. A few weeks before, the staff had asked what we intended doing on 31 December ... what were our plans? We said, 'Well it is New Year's Eve. What do you mean? What are our plans? Do you want balloons and things?'

They said, 'No. We want to be assured that the restaurant will not open on that evening. It is a religious holiday for us.'

We were a bit put out about this. We thought it was unlikely to be a religious holiday but we ought to make inquiries. Of course it was nonsense.

We explained that New Year's Eve was the one night when everyone in Britain went out. We simply had to be open. But they were not at all happy. They told us that friends of theirs in other restaurants in Chelsea were having the night off. Eventually they agreed to meet us half-way. They would be on duty and serve a limited menu provided they were allowed to wear fancy dress.

We thought this might be rather fun and agreed. As a parting shot, I remember one of the waiters shouted after us as we were leaving the restaurant, 'You are wrong, you know. No one will come here on New Year's Eve.'

And he was right. When we went along, the place was practically empty. There were just a few of the old ladies living in Markham Square there having a quiet dinner ... the very ones, no doubt, who had supported the Chelsea Society so loudly and objected so vehemently to what we were doing at Markham House. We discovered that night that whilst an awful lot of people do go out, these people go to ritzy places like the Savoy where they have a midnight cabaret and balloons and whistles or else they stay at home and have a private party. The only people who go to a place like Alexander's on such a night are those who have nowhere else to go. Alexander and I were thankful that we had invited two guests to be with us ... Terry Hooper and Sarah Rothschild. It turned out to be a very odd dinner party. And a very odd night altogether.

The waiters were in full drag ... the most tremendous drag you can imagine. They were dressed in women's clothes, wearing false eyelashes, tiaras, jewels, goodness knows what. One of them was impersonating Anna Magnani with huge false bosoms.

Fortunately, the old ladies simply hadn't a clue what it was all about. They sat quietly eating their dinner with half a glass of wine to celebrate the New Year, apparently completely unconscious that anything unusual was going on.

Later, the place became crowded with French and Italians ... friends of the waiters who had the night off. One of them worked at Buckingham Palace and arrived in what was said to be one of the Queen's dresses and wearing a tiara.

Then the most beautiful boy, fantastically slim and elegant, walked in. He swept down the stairs wearing a marvellous white satin ball dress with a full train and tiara. He had a white mink wrap round his shoulders. He looked like the most marvellous model girl. We found out that his photograph had, in fact, appeared many times in a famous fashion magazine, showing hats. I imagine that the Editor never knew who the model was.

It was the fullest, wildest drag I've ever seen in my life. La Dolce Vita wasn't in it! The four of us were bewitched – and speechless!

We couldn't believe it!

Fortunately before the boys started going really wild, the old ladies went home. And the cabaret turns came on. They all joined in a can-can demonstration and when it came to the uproarious climax of the whole thing, one of them, dancing on the bar top, bent over and threw up his skirts as the real can-can girls do. He had a lighted candle thrust in his bottom! How he had managed to keep it alight under his skirts, I can't think!

We were getting really frightened by this time. We thought that any minute the police might see what was going on from the pavement outside and come in. We knew they would have the place closed. But we couldn't do anything. The whole thing was out of control. We couldn't cope.

Finally we got up and ran away.

In those early days it seemed that we were always trying to control people without much success … people we employed but who were often much more adult than we were. We really had no idea how to do it. They knew so much more than we did.

It could be that this was one reason why the restaurant was so successful. We were lucky in that the head waiter and the two chefs were really marvellous and they did keep the inevitable cheating that always goes on in this kind of business within reasonable limits. We knew perfectly well that butter and sugar and coffee were going out regularly to families and grandmothers but it was on a reasonable scale. The sort of thing that can ruin any restaurant is the wholesale disappearance of gallons of oil and bottles of wines and spirits. This didn't happen. If it had, we could not have survived. There were still times when we were terribly pushed for ready money.

It was one of these times when Alexander, Archie and I, sitting in the restaurant having a late lunch and working on accounts long after the place emptied in the afternoon, suddenly saw two men coming down the outside stairs. We recognized them at once; they were from the butcher who was supplying all the meat to the restaurant. We knew our account was overdue but we hadn't a hope of paying till the end of the month.

Alexander and Archie shot into the back kitchens and put on the chefs white coats and caps and came out behind the counter. They put on a great show of whipping up eggs and heating the omelette pan while I sat at the table sipping campari and trying to look like an impatient customer having a late meal and still waiting for my omelette.

They both pretended to be Italian and unable to understand one word of English. The poor wretched bill collectors stood there saying over and over again that unless the account was settled at once, no more meat would be delivered. Archie and Alexander just smiled and nodded their heads and at intervals said such things as ... *"scusa ... no comprendo ... no speaka da English ... stupido ..."*

Finally they gave it up as a bad job and went away.

It may be difficult to understand how we could still be so short of ready cash because both Alexander's and Bazaar made profits from the start. The thing is that however much money you take in a business like a restaurant or a boutique, this has to be spent right away on keeping the thing going. I know we didn't manage things very well. Our banking was done in a very odd way. We had a drawer in a table at the back of Bazaar and all the money we took was put in here. When we couldn't shut the drawer, we collected everything in it and went out and banked it. This might happen once a month by which time there could be something like three to four thousand pounds in the drawer in cheques and cash. We probably lost quite a bit of money or it got stolen.

We had the most peculiar way of paying our accounts, too. We did not know anything about invoices and statements or the difference between them. We kept all the bills that came in in one big pile and when the pile looked too monstrous, Alexander would sit down, get out the Company's cheque book and, taking a bill from the top of the pile, start writing. The result was that some bills were paid over and over again and some poor people never got any money at all if their invoice, or statement, or whatever, happened to be at the bottom of the pile.

I must say people are astonishingly honest. We were constantly having cheques returned to us with a note saying the account had already been paid. We kept no records at all. That is, until Archie spotted all this and came in and put a bit of sense into our accounting system.

The big day of the week at Bazaar has always been Saturday. There are still Saturdays when we have to keep the door locked and let one customer in as another goes out. We are terribly cramped for space and the sort of things we sell take up a lot of display room and bring in a lot of people.

For instance, one of our most successful early lines was the little white plastic collar that is supposed to make all the difference to a rather dreary black sweater or dress. We sold these at two-and-six each and we sold literally thousands and thousands of them.

If you think how many things like this have to be sold to make up the hundreds of pounds a day we were taking, you will understand how crowded the place would become. And Alexander and I were the only 'sales'. Archie would come in and help when he could but he still had his own businesses – the coffee bar and his photography studio called Alistair Jourdan – to look after and, in addition, he was now doing all our books.

One Saturday afternoon when we were almost demented trying to keep everyone happy, Kay Kendall walked in, her six pugs on six individual leads with her. The confusion was awful. She always had these six dogs with her and on this particular Saturday, when all the changing rooms were already full and we had one customer using our office and another monopolizing the lavatory as changing rooms, the pugs seemed to be everywhere. Each one wanted to go in a different direction. It was pandemonium.

Alexander tried to look after Kay Kendall as he knew her slightly. She chose some dresses and then said, 'I can't wait. You'll have to find somewhere for me to try these on at once.'

In desperation, Alexander suggested the restaurant. 'We can take the dresses down there if you like,' he said.

They marched out of the door together, Alexander carrying the dresses she had chosen over his arm and the dogs all tangled up in his legs. They went down to the restaurant, turned on the lights and, while Alexander was hanging the clothes over the backs of chairs, Kay took her clothes off. It didn't take long. She had no bra, no knickers. She was completely naked under the dress she was wearing. It was a bit disconcerting for Alexander but he tried hard to appear unmoved as he handed her one dress after another gazing nonchalantly – he hoped – out of the window. Then something caught his eye. Framed in the dark window looking in on the brightly lit restaurant were two small boys. Obviously they had seen the great film star come out of Bazaar and go downstairs to the restaurant and they thought this a wonderful chance to get her autograph. They were peering in, completely engrossed in all that was going on. When they saw that Alexander had spotted them, they turned without making a sound, their mouths still wide open in wonder, and simply shot up the stairs and disappeared.

Meantime, Kay Kendall went on calmly trying on the dresses. She bought four of them.

One Friday night, rather late, Alexander was just about to close up shop when a rather large lady walked in. She looked slightly arch and a bit skittish when she said to Alexander, 'I hear you have some rather good black tights. I believe they are the thing in Chelsea, aren't they? I am going to a Chelsea party tonight. Have you any that will fit me?'

We were selling these black stretch tights like hot cakes and we had quite a big supply of them but Alexander didn't really think we had any that would fit this customer. Avoiding the direct issue, he said, 'We have them in thirty-four, thirty-six and thirty-eight-inch hip sizes and they do stretch.'

Rather coyly, she replied, 'I'm afraid I may be bigger than that!'

And Alexander, trying to be helpful, said, 'But they do stretch, madam.'

'Do you think black tights will look all right on me?' she persisted.

'Yes, of course,' replied Alexander who by this time regarded the whole thing as something of a game and felt sure that after all this, she would buy a box at least.

'Can I try them on?'

'Yes, do!'

She disappeared into the changing room and put them on. When she came out, she said, 'How do I look?'

'All right,' said Alexander. (When he was telling me about it, he said that in fact they did not look awfully good!)

But the customer had not finished yet.

'You are a very tall young man,' she said. 'I am rather short. How do I look to you from that height?'

Alexander, who by this time was playing up, said, 'Men like me like girls with a bit of ...'

'Does my bottom look too large?'

'Of course not. Bottoms can never look too large for me.'

Alexander was overdoing it. He was thinking of the whole thing as a game to humour a child. The customer was enjoying it. She went on, 'I am told there is a lot of sitting down at parties like the one I am going to. Would you mind sitting down? I will walk past you and you can tell me what you think.'

Alexander sat down on a chair and she walked to and fro. A bit worn by now, he said, 'You look fine to me ... absolutely fine.'

Perhaps he said this too enthusiastically. She went back into the attack.

'I am told that at Chelsea parties people even lie on the floor. I shall have to walk past them. I wonder if you would mind ...'

This was too much. Alexander got up from the chair and went back behind the counter. He had had enough. He wasn't having any more. Fortunately she got the message. She would have liked to walk out of the shop without buying a thing but she didn't dare. She bought one pair of black stretch tights ... thirty-nine and elevenpence.

We had another rather ghastly experience but at least on this occasion we were all together. We were visited by a well-known international crook and his blonde girl friend. Of course we had no idea who he was when he came in though he certainly looked the part, sitting back with a thumb stuck in his rather loud waist-coat pocket and smoking a big and expensive cigar.

We were excited when we first saw these two because it was so obvious that here was the rich boy friend anxious to buy his blonde everything she wanted. They were just getting down to it ... the girl wanting everything she saw ... when a friend of Archie's walked into the shop.

He took Archie aside into the office.

'You know who you have got there?' he said. 'His cheques bounce. He's well known for it. He just leaves the country and disappears. Watch out!'

I knew by Archie's manner when he rejoined us that something was wrong. Hour after hour went by and the pile of dresses the blonde wanted kept on mounting. The value of the things put on one side for her went up from one hundred pounds to two hundred and from two to three and finally to four hundred pounds.

Even the boy friend was beginning to look a bit anxious.

'Do you think you really need that?' he asked once or twice. 'Don't you think that one rather overlaps those you have already chosen?'

Meantime, Archie's nervousness had communicated itself to me. I could see that he was trying to get rid of the two of them.

If we had had a telephone working that day, I think I would probably have made some sort of excuse and phoned the police. But it had been disconnected. Probably the telephone account was at the bottom of the pile of invoices and bills in the office.

It was after closing time ... nearly seven o'clock ... far too late to get in touch with the bank if a cheque was produced. We simply could not afford to lose all the dresses we would normally expect to sell in a day. How were we going to refuse a cheque? I could see that Archie was getting really worked up because it was his responsibility.

To ward off the awful moment which by this time we all felt sure was coming, Archie got out the drinks. We started playing for time not knowing what on earth we were going to do with it anyway.

Then, suddenly, this man put his hand in his pocket. I am not sure what I expected ... a gun or a cheque book. Neither came out. Instead he produced the most enormous wad of notes. He simply peeled off the fivers. He paid the whole lot in cash.

What a moment that was! He got to be rather a friend of ours.

That's just one of our sticky experiences. Another was the robbery. This happened one evening when we were working late because the new collection was to be delivered from the workroom. A good few people knew that we expected it because we were so excited about the new designs that we couldn't stop talking about them.

For some reason, the delivery was late. Alexander and Archie and I went next door to the Markham Arms to have a drink. As we walked out of Bazaar we noticed that there seemed to be an unusual number of people standing around but this did not make any great impression on us at the time. We had one drink then Archie left because he wanted to get home. Alexander and I had one more and ten minutes after Archie left … it certainly wasn't any longer … we went back to Bazaar. In our brief absence, the place had been ransacked. There wasn't a thing left. Every garment … every single belt and scarf and collar … had been taken. Even the hangers had been pinched.

If the new collection had been there, as it had been promised and as we expected it to be, we would have been ruined. We simply had not enough capital for another collection.

Transport problems saved us that time!

I don't think this robbery was planned with the idea of ruining us. We all believe it was probably someone's idea of a joke. But when the police came and started questioning us, the whole pattern of events began to piece itself together.

A couple of days earlier, a man had come into the shop and asked Alexander if he might take photographs. He said, 'I am taking photographs of people well known in the King's Road and would like to have some of you in Bazaar.'

This was rather flattering and appeared to be reasonable enough. Alexander agreed. Photographs of him in every part of the shop were taken. It only occurred to us when we were talking to the police that these must have been part of the plan. With these photographs whoever was planning the operation could explain every detail of the layout of the place and time the whole thing to a split second.

It was all done in the ten minutes we were in the Markham Arms. The lock had not been forced. Whoever broke in had a skeleton key. And this had been used to lock up again when the job was done.

Archie remembered that when he had left, he had noticed a couple of taxis parked at the corner of the square with the 'hired' flags down. He also said that he had had the impression that he was escorted home by someone tailing his footsteps. But none of this helped.

When we worked it out, we realized that at least six people must have been involved. The moment we were seen going into the Markham Arms, they must have moved in and systematically removed everything in the place putting the whole lot into the taxis waiting outside.

The odd thing was that not a single one of the garments stolen was ever seen again and this was rather remarkable because at that time my clothes seemed so way-out that they were immediately recognizable. Maybe the robbers – whoever they were – just ditched the lot!

Fortunately there had been very little cash in the till ... about fifteen pounds. Alexander hoped to cause dissension in the gang by saying there was a great deal more than this. He knew there was no question of misleading the insurance company people because loose cash was not covered by our policy so he was not letting them in for anything which had not, in fact, been stolen. But he reckoned that if the gang heard there had been between two and three hundred pounds in the till and they had been told there was only fifteen pounds, this might start something. They'd think they had been cheated by the man who organized the whole thing and might start beefing about it. But we have no idea if this worked. I hope so. The whole thing is still an unsolved mystery.

Shortly after this episode, Archie got married. He bought a house and let me have his flat in the King's Road. This was quite something. It was the first time I had had a flat that I could think of as a home. It was absolutely marvellous.

I moved in during Christmas week and on Christmas Eve I decided to give my first party. Alexander and I invited Terry Hooper, who was – and still is – a terrific friend, and a slightly mad Australian girl to join us.

Terry is a great cook; at one time he helped out at Alexander's restaurant as chef. He said he would cook our Christmas dinner.

The evening started in tremendous style but we got rather behind with the cooking arrangements. It was one o'clock in the morning before dinner was ready.

We all ate the delicious swan I had been sold in lieu of the goose I thought I had ordered and felt most splendidly at peace with the world afterwards. Then suddenly it began to snow. We were all probably rather drunk by this time and stood around the window gazing out at the King's Road which was so much a part of our lives. We were maudlin and near to tears.

Then Alexander said, 'We can't … we simply can't … stay here. It is Christmas and it is snowing. Let's go out and find real snow. Where shall we go?'

We all produced suggestions of one kind and another but Alexander said, 'No.'

Suddenly he turned to us. 'How much money have we got between us?' he asked.

We searched around and found we had about twenty pounds all told.

'That's no good,' he said. 'We will have to go over to Alexander's and see what's in the till. First, let's all get our passports.'

We piled into the Bentley outside (it was one Alexander had been lent by a friend) and rushed round collecting passports. Then we went to Alexander's restaurant. We found about a hundred and fifty pounds in the till. We took it and put an I.O.U. in its place for Archie. Then we went upstairs to Bazaar. We found two hundred pounds there. We went on to the Fantasy and collected a further hundred. Alexander had all the keys and everywhere we went we left I.O.U.s and a note explaining that we'd borrowed the money.

We drove to London Airport. We were all in evening dress. I had pulled on a huge sweater and fortunately this had an enormous pocket across the front rather like a kangaroo's pouch. We stuffed all the fivers, pounds and ten shilling notes we'd collected into this pocket. I looked at least six months pregnant.

At the Airport, Alexander went straight over to the ticket desk. 'Where's the next plane going to?' he asked.

The man said, 'Where do you want to go, sir?'

'We don't care. We want to be on the next flight.'

We must have looked a highly suspicious bunch of characters but we were given tickets, told we would be going to Zürich and, as there was no one else around, we walked straight through the Customs.

We arrived at Zürich at about six o'clock on Christmas Day morning feeling simply awful. We were in evening dress; we had hangovers; we hadn't a toothbrush between us, and we were frozen.

After a while Alexander managed to hire a car with a most efficient heater and we got into this quickly and shut every possible crack of ventilation. We drove ... and drove ... and drove. We drove all through Christmas Day and night. We drove through Boxing Day. We were on the road swerving round the most ghastly icy mountain passes for more than thirty hours. At one point while driving along the edge of a precipice, Alexander dropped his lighted cigarette and it fell inside his trousers where a fly button had come off. In his anxiety to protect his manhood he lost control of the car for a moment and we were jolly nearly killed.

We arrived at Davos late on Boxing Day in evening dress and absolutely exhausted. We had loads and loads of money ... I was weighed down with the stuff ... but we had no clothes!

What we wanted more than anything else was a hot meal. Davos was full of holiday-makers and we found we could not get in to any of the nice-looking restaurants. Perhaps they did not care for the look of us, which was not surprising. Eventually we found a *pension* with a restaurant attached. We went in and because it was Boxing Day we decided we would be rather grand and order *à la carte*.

We were just beginning to relax in the warmth of the place, drinking the wine and wolfing the bread on the table and gloating on the prospect of food in the immediate future, when suddenly the place became absolutely full of people. Obviously they were all residents and the gong had sounded! Immediately they sat down, dinner was put in front of them. We were ignored. And we were ravenous! We sat for an hour, the hunger pangs getting worse and worse with every minute. It was too much for Terry. Suddenly he was really furious. He got up. 'Let's get out of here,' he said.

We all got up and prepared to leave. Immediately the proprietress sprang up from behind the cash desk and came over to us. At the top of her voice she screamed, 'You have ordered an expensive dinner. You must stay and have it.'

Terry said firmly, 'No. We have waited an hour and we have not even been given the cold things we ordered to start our meal. I quite understand your difficulty with all these regular customers to feed but you could at least have given us our *pâté* and toast and *hors d'oeuvre*. We are leaving.'

'You shan't leave!' she screamed. 'You can leave only if you pay.'

'We have no intention of paying,' Alexander said, by now in his most dignified and arrogant mood. 'If you have any complaint I suggest you telephone for the police.'

The proprietress rushed over to the door and bolted it. We sat down again. Almost immediately it seemed as if we were surrounded by a lot of thugs who stood around in a menacing way. We thought they were going to beat us up but fortunately they didn't. Instead we managed to persuade one of them to telephone the police.

The police arrived. They listened to both sides of the story. But it was all too confused. They really had very little idea of what it was all about. As a precaution, they arrested Alexander, presumably as a hostage, and took him off to the local police station where he had to spend the rest of the week. They confiscated all our passports.

Terry and the Australian girl and I had to find a hotel and make the best of it. To pass the time we hired ourselves terribly chic ski clothes, went ski-ing with an instructor every day and visited Alexander in prison whenever we were allowed to. He was not put in a cell; in fact, the Swiss police were rather charming to him; he had quite a nice room at the station.

He was absolutely determined that we were not going to pay that bill. He got rather pompous about the whole thing. The police did their best to persuade him to change his mind. They told us that it would be three months before our case was likely to come up before the courts and that unless we paid we could not be allowed to leave the country.

Alexander insisted that this was a civil dispute and that the police had no right to hold him or any one of us. He played on their feelings shamelessly; he kept telling them that the publicity in Britain that would inevitably be given to such a case as ours would certainly go against their tourist industry.

'British people simply won't come to a country where visitors are treated in this way,' he said.

Eventually he persuaded them to allow him to engage an attorney. This man turned out to be a very clever and understanding type and Alexander convinced him that we felt we had been cheated.

'Purely on a moral basis, payment of such a bill as this is out of the question,' Alexander said. 'We are determined not to pay. And equally determined to fight the case if necessary.' Alexander briefed this attorney so well and so convincingly that he was able to persuade the police to release him and return our passports. There was some sort of understanding that we would all meet the next day but Alexander had the feeling that the attorney did not expect us to keep this appointment. He – and the police – by this time wanted to get us out of the country and let the whole thing drop.

We all piled into the car, left the money to pay our hotel bill, the attorney's account and all we owed for the hire of skis and ski clothes in addressed envelopes and set out for Zürich.

We arrived there on New Year's Eve. We were wearing the evening clothes we had put on in London on Christmas Eve. Words cannot describe what we must have looked like!

We found that New Year's Eve in a Swiss airport is a time of celebration. There was a giant Christmas tree in the lounge and the whole place was swarming with slightly drunk officials. They began throwing their weight around and making rude suggestions. I had taken my shoes off because I was so tired. These were immediately pinched and hidden. One official put his arm round me and gave me a smacking kiss.

This was too much for Alexander and Terry. Suddenly they saw it all as a challenge. It was impossible to start a free-for-all fight; there were far too many of them. Instead, Alexander and Terry started talking to these men, two at a time. They said something like, 'You look an intelligent sort of man. Would you mind coming behind the Christmas tree where it is quiet so we can talk for a moment.'

These men fell for this. The moment they were behind the tree and out of sight of the other, Alexander and Terry took on one each and sloshed them. Bang!

Alexander always says he is a frightful coward but on this night he was very brave. So was Terry, who is much smaller. Fortunately these officials were ghastly cowards and they were so taken by surprise and so off-guard that they went down one by one.

Goodness knows what would have happened if this had gone on but fortunately our flight was called, and with the automatic response to discipline which seems to be inherent in the Swiss, all the officials rallied. They appeared to sober up immediately in a flash.

We realized that we were in a frightfully difficult position. I didn't wait to find my shoes. We ran out across the tarmac towards the plane that was waiting. We ran very fast; we were really quite frightened. There were about fifteen of these very angry officials chasing us.

We bundled up the steps of the plane somehow and, when our eyes became accustomed to the lights, we suddenly realized we were in a cabin full of Indians. The plane had come from Karachi and stopped at Zürich en route for London. Inside, it was a blazing mass of exotic colours; the women in gorgeous saris, the men in elaborate turbans. After what we had just gone through it gave us a terrific shock. It didn't seem real.

We were just about to plonk into seats, full of relief that we'd got away at last and were on the way home when one of the crew came along and said he was awfully sorry but the Captain had seen what had been happening on the tarmac and could not allow us to fly with him. We argued with a desperate anxiety but it was no good. The Captain insisted that he would not have trouble makers on his plane. We could not blame him. It was obvious that he had seen the rearguard action Alexander and Terry had been fighting as we ran towards the plane.

We were practically pushed off ... fairly shovelled down the steps into the arms of what appeared to us to be a mob of angry antagonists waiting to lynch us. Fortunately they didn't seem to realize that Terry's girl friend was with us. Obviously they thought she had been caught up in the disturbance we had created by accident. They allowed her to remain on board which was just as well as she had been away from her office for over a week without permission and was feeling rather desperate about the whole thing. To help her, we pretended she wasn't with us.

The curious thing was that the Swiss officials, seeing us being thrown out so unceremoniously, suddenly had a change of heart. Perhaps their sentimentality got the better of them. Anyway it appeared that they thought we were probably all right after all. They seemed to forget what had gone before and became desperately concerned about the loss of my shoes. They were frightfully upset about the whole thing. They seemed to be indignant about what they had seen. Such a thing had never happened in their airport; they had never seen British people thrown off a flight before.

They began rushing round talking of special flights. Heaven knows how they fixed it but after about three hours a plane of the Swiss Air Force (which, frankly, we hadn't even known existed) arrived and the pilot took us to Basle. When we got there, he found another pilot willing to take us on a little further and finally we landed at Paris.

We were given V.I.P. treatment all the way. They gave us champagne and escorted us off the plane first when we reached Orly.

A jeep was waiting to rush us to Le Bourget so that we could catch the next plane to London.

I don't like to think what we must have looked like. We had been wearing evening clothes practically continuously for eight days. On top of these we now had the thick sweaters we had bought in Davos. We must have looked grotesque. Still, we had learned to ski … at least, Terry and I had. Alexander had been far too busy practising his legal talents.

It was after this adventure, and perhaps inspired by the awful time Archie had when he found we had evaporated leaving nothing behind to give any clue but a string of I.O.U.s, that we came to two big decisions. Archie decided to sell the Fantasy and give all his time to the fashion business; and we decided to sell the restaurant.

We sold Alexander's for two reasons. The chief one was the rate at which Bazaar was expanding. Archie and Alexander and I all realized that we would have to concentrate all our efforts on this. The other was the fact that we heard several of the staff discussing the possibilities of opening up places of their own.

We had noticed that our waiters and chefs had begun to turn up driving outrageously grand Mercedes and Alfa Romeo cars. Most of them were, in fact, the sons of frightfully rich Italian families who had left Italy for some reason or another and, having been out of their own country for three years or so, were now able to withdraw large sums of capital. We knew perfectly well that the basic reason for the tremendous success of Alexander's was the staff. They were all loyal and hardworking. We realized that if we had to replace them, the whole thing might end up a failure. It is a tricky thing running a restaurant profitably largely because of the wholesale pilfering that goes on. We had some experience of this when we opened a second restaurant which was called Plunket's which had to be closed after about a year because of this. It was a complete write-off.

If the staff we had left Alexander's it would virtually mean starting all over again. We really hadn't time to do this. The three of us decided that the best thing would be to offer the place to them. We knew they had the money to buy it; they knew better than anyone else exactly what the place was worth because they knew what the takings were; and we knew they wanted a place of their own.

The deal went through very simply and Archie, Alexander and I were completely free to concentrate on the building of Bazaar. It had begun to dawn on us that by luck ... by chance ... perhaps even by mistake ... we were on to a huge thing. We were in at the beginning of a tremendous renaissance in fashion. It was not happening because of us. It was simply that, as things turned out, we were a part of it.

There was hardly a day when Chelsea was not mentioned or featured in one way or another in the newspapers. Chelsea suddenly became Britain's San Francisco, Greenwich Village and the Left Bank. The Press publicized its cellars, its beat joints, its girls and their clothes. Chelsea ceased to be a small part of London; it became international; its name interpreted a way of living and a way of dressing far more than a geographical area.

The Chelsea girl, the original leather-booted, black-stockinged girl who came out of the King's Road looking like some contemporary counterpart of a gay musketeer, began to be copied by the rest of London and watched with interest by others all over the country. Soon the 'look' was to be copied internationally. This girl's challenging clothes were accepted as a challenge. It was she who established the fact that this latter half of the twentieth century belongs to Youth.

She was heavily criticized by many but entirely vindicated I thought by the American journalist, John Crosby, who wrote in the New York *Herald Tribune*, 'The English girl has an enthusiasm that American men find utterly captivating. I'd like to export the whole Chelsea girl with her "life is fabulous" philosophy to America with instructions to bore from within ... to spread the subversive word that being a girl is a much more rewarding occupation than being a Lady Senator or even a Lady President.'

Over and over again I was told I was responsible for the off-beat clothes that became known as the Chelsea Look. I heard my clothes described as dishy, grotty, geary, kinky, mod, poove and all the rest of it. People either loved or hated them. But, in fact, no one designer is ever responsible for such a revolution. All a designer can do is to anticipate a mood before people realize that they are bored with what they have already got. It is simply a question of who gets bored first. Fortunately I am apt to get bored pretty quickly. Perhaps this is the essence of designing.

Lord Northcliffe said that an influential newspaper can amplify a swing of public opinion but can do nothing to reverse it. This is as true of fashion as it is of journalism.

Good designers – like clever newspapermen – know that to have any influence they must keep in step with public needs … public opinion … and that intangible 'something in the air'. They must catch the spirit of the day and interpret it in clothes before other designers begin to twitch at the nerve ends.

I just happened to start when that 'something in the air' was coming to the boil. The clothes I made happened to fit in exactly with the teenage trend, with pop records and espresso bars and jazz clubs. The rejuvenated *Queen* magazine, *Beyond the Fringe*, *Private Eye*, the discotheques and *That Was the Week That Was* were all born on the same wavelength.

Never before have the young set the pace as they do now. Never before have so many of the leaders, the trend-setters in all fields of design, been so young. And dress design is not only the most significant and speediest of the decorative arts, it is also the most important because it is so personal. Clothes are not only necessary for warmth and decency but are also an essential factor in the delicate art of putting oneself across … socially, professionally and commercially. Trend-setting demands confidence as well as perseverance. But, more than anything else, it demands a flair for choosing a look that will catch on despite all initial opposition.

Once only the rich, the Establishment, set the fashion. Now it is the inexpensive little dress seen on the girls in the High Street. These girls may have their faults. Often they may be too opinionated and extravagant. But the important thing is that they are alive … looking, listening, ready to try anything new.

It is their questioning attitude which makes them important and different. They conform to their own set of values but not to the values and standards laid down by a past generation. But they don't sneer at other points of view. If they don't wish to campaign against the Bomb, they don't sneer at those who do. They are not silly or flirtatious or militant. Being militant and aggressive is as ridiculous to them as being coy and deliberately seductive. They make no pretensions.

Sex is taken for granted. They talk candidly about everything from puberty to homosexuality. The girls are curiously feminine but their femininity lies in their attitude rather than in their appearance. They may be dukes' daughters, doctors' daughters or dockers' daughters. They are not interested in status symbols. They don't worry about accents or class; they are neither determinedly county nor working-class. They are scornful of pretence of any kind.

There was a time when clothes were a sure sign of a woman's social position and income group. Not now. Snobbery has gone out of fashion, and in our shops you will find duchesses jostling with typists to buy the same dresses.

Once upon a time if two women turned up at a party wearing the same dress, it wrecked the party. There were hysterical outbursts and one of them probably walked out. Nowadays, it is not unusual to see several identical dresses at the same party and the girls love it. You can see them huddling together, delighted at this confirmation of their own good taste. At Washington's Opera Ball this year, I believe there were fifteen or twenty identical or indistinguishable dresses and the hostess, the French Ambassador's wife, Mme Herve Alpand, said she thought it gave 'a kick to the ball – in a nice way, of course'.

The voices, rules and culture of this generation are as different from those of the past as tea and wine. And the clothes they choose evoke their lives ... daring and gay, never dull.

They think for themselves. They are committed and involved. Prejudices no longer exist. They represent the whole new spirit that is present-day Britain, a classless spirit that has grown out of the Second World War.

They will not accept truisms or propaganda. They are superbly international. The same clothes are worn in Britain, Europe and America. The same sort of food is eaten, too. I think there may be a chance that you can't swing a war on a generation which does not think in terms of 'us' against the foreigners.

The young will not be dictated to. You can be publicized on the national network television programmes, be written up by the most famous of the fashion columnists and the garment still won't sell if the young don't like it.

I admire them tremendously.

These girls may start as the ones who fill the coffee bars in worn jeans, dirty duffle coats and with uncombed hair but they can change – almost overnight. They are the Mods. At first glance the uninitiated may find it hard to tell the sexes apart. The traditional symbols have gone. Brilliant colour is today as permissible in men's wear as it is in women's. Long and short hair cuts are worn by both. Since the sexes live much the same sort of lives, they want the same sort of clothes to live them in.

It is the Mods … the direct opposite of the Rockers (who seem to be anti-everything) … who gave the dress trade the impetus to break through the fast-moving, breathtaking, up-rooting revolution in which we have played a part since the opening of Bazaar.

We had to keep up with them. We had to expand. This would not have been possible if Archie had not decided to come in with us. We needed his full-time help badly. A clever accountant is absolutely essential to a growing business. Costing is vitally important and terribly complicated … far too complicated for the untrained brain. We had managed to learn a little from our early battles with the trade over under-pricing but not nearly enough.

Costing is a talent in its own right. It is like the most nerve-racking gamble in the world. When you start to cost a dress you have got to find out first whether you can get the right quantity of material at the right price. Then you have got to work out just how much all the things that go into the finished dress are going to cost. The whole thing is wide open to doubt all the way through.

In theory it should be easy enough but dresses have to be made in different sizes and obviously large ones take more cloth than small.

Then you have got to have a rough idea of how many of each garment you are going to sell because in costing all the overheads, the expense of the original pattern, the machinists and the workrooms, have to be taken into account and a proportion of these allocated to each garment.

One might think that the answer is simply to work on the basis that the worst is going to happen. But, if you do this, the worst will happen because the price will be far too high.

Then, just as you think you're getting somewhere, the price of the cloth you have planned to use shoots up. The more you think about it, the more terrifying the whole thing becomes. If, in fact, we estimate that we will sell 750 of a particular dress and we are wrong and only a hundred are sold either because it is not a good dress or for some reason it does not catch the eye of the buyers or of the fashion Press, we are in frightful trouble.

Obviously far too much cloth has been ordered. And we are stuck with it. Sometimes it may be possible to bring back a certain cloth into a later collection after an interval of time but, meantime, one's money is locked up in stock that is dormant and doing nothing more than take up a lot of storage space.

You never really get your money back. The best you can hope for is to recoup some of the losses. And the more you try to be ahead of fashion, the more publicity you get, the more likely this sort of thing is to happen.

It is impossible to predict which one of the dresses in a new collection will be the one the fashion girls will pick on. In fact, you can never count on any publicity at all. And – if it comes – it can be a double-edged weapon.

Undoubtedly publicity makes a difference to sales … they shoot up right away … but it also makes the look, the line and the design known all over the country so you have got to finish it quickly before the cheap copies in inferior material are all over the place.

The problem always is that if you start a distinctive trend in fashion, you are also digging its grave right from the beginning because the more people are converted to your way of dress, the less exclusive it becomes and a uniform is born.

I don't want my clothes to be anything like a uniform. I believe clothes should be a background to personality. The dress should attract attention from across a room but, close to, no one should be distracted from the person by the dress. The only answer, from a designer's point of view, is a new collection every season with a new look which should develop and evolve naturally out of the fashion line that is on its way out.

We were beginning to get some sort of professional organization into the daily running of Bazaar when we got a letter from David Wynne Morgan. He has made a speciality of overseas fashion trips. Up to date I believe he has been responsible for the organization of something like a hundred of these showing British fashions all over Europe and in many other parts of the world, too.

On this particular occasion, he was putting on a show at the Palace Hotel, St Moritz. The grandees of the British fashion world like Victor Stiebel, Mattli, John Cavanagh and Worth were all sending a part of their latest collections. David wanted to include a few items from Bazaar.

I really think that his idea behind this was to give the show a bit of comic relief. He thought the whole operation was beginning to show signs of growing too grand for words. He wanted my things to add a bit of zip. From our point of view, this was splendid. It was putting Bazaar right up amongst the top bracket at a time when my clothes were still considered pretty crazy outside Chelsea. The things I was making had nothing to do with accepted couture.

We had a nightmare time trying to get everything ready. The red tape, when you take fashion clothes out of this country, even when the sole idea is to stimulate overseas interest in Britain, is quite fantastic. Everything has to be described in the minutest detail and sent 'in bond' with the guarantee that nothing will be sold and everything will come back into this country exactly as it leaves it. The official forms are endless. We all went mad trying to satisfy the customs people.

So many things go to make up an outfit of mine. One Norfolk jacket with fur collar, one pair of knickerbockers, one pair of knee socks, one pair of knee-high boots, one fur hat … all these for just one outfit and every detail had to be entered in triplicate, the materials described and each item individually weighed. It cannot have been nearly so difficult for the couture people … a ball gown or a mink coat is easy to detail in comparison.

All the clothes to be shown were supposed to be sent out to St Moritz in advance. Of course my things weren't ready in time. I was so excited that I kept thinking of something new I simply had to have. We sent all we had ready with the others but because of all my last minute ideas, I had to take at least half our collection with me as personal luggage.

The trouble was that we hadn't got enough suitcases. All we could find at the last minute were odd cardboard boxes … commercial crates we begged from our grocer, covered with advertising slogans like The Milky Way and Eat Mars Bars and that sort of thing. We had to tie these up with string. It was all very undignified. It looked horribly slap-dash and amateur specially when I found myself at London Airport in my leather coat and black stockings and black boots surrounded by the most fantastic girls you can imagine.

The models chosen for the trip were the absolute tops. It was the beginning of the craze for wigs and since the idea was to get as much publicity as possible, they were all wearing great peruke things … very elaborate … specially made for the occasion by John Olofson of Knightsbridge. It was an extraordinary sight. Nine absolutely gorgeous girls in these amazing wigs and wearing magnificent mink coats practically down to the ankles.

We had to travel first by air, then by train and more train. It was an exhausting journey and on the way I started to develop the most awful flu. It got worse and worse by the hour. I was practically dead when we finally arrived at the Palace Hotel where the skiers who want to see and be seen by royalty and the millionaires go.

Walking into the palatial foyer of the Hotel, where the atmosphere is still one of Edwardian pomp and circumstance, with all these gorgeous girls and with what looked like mountains of luggage, the scene must have recalled to old stagers there the palmy days before World War I when the Maharaja of Hyderabad would arrive with five hundred trunks and a personal cook to sprinkle gold dust on his curry.

Those days have gone but the Palace Hotel still has the reputation of being the one place where on the register the word most frequently written under the heading 'occupation' is the self-assured 'none' of the unashamed aristocrat. It still has something like sixty thousand bottles in its wine cellars and it still keeps goodness knows how many live trout in its fish tanks; it is still the place where poodles wear mink when they go out in the snow for their daily walk.

It was the height of the season between Christmas Eve and New Year. The hotel was full. The girls were all put in a sort of dormitory together but, because of some misunderstanding in the bookings, there wasn't a room for me. No one at the hotel had the slightest idea who I was. By this time I was feeling really ghastly and was thankful when a sort of box room with a bed was discovered empty. It was very tiny but at that moment I wanted no more than a bed.

When the girls went down to dinner, I was too exhausted to go with them but I knew I had to eat if I was to be able to work in the morning. I decided to have some dinner in bed. This wasn't too easy. When dinner is served in a private room at the Palace Hotel, it is served with great ceremony.

Three rather gorgeous-looking waiters arrived, each carrying a great silver tray. They did their best to get into my room to serve the elaborate food in the manner in which they had been so carefully schooled. It just was not possible. They had to come in one at a time, deposit the food on the bed, turn round and get out before the next one could enter.

I managed to get up in the morning and for two days and most of the nights we rehearsed solidly. All the grand clothes and the mink coats had to be fitted into some sort of coherent sequence and we had to decide on the right moment for Bazaar to make its appearance.

In order to save money, David had not organized professional dressers until the actual night so, for the rehearsals, I acted as dresser and worked with David. I still had a high temperature and was in a pretty dotty state.

It was an elaborate show to put on. Seeing the girls parade in the magnificent ball gowns of the haute couture with millionaire minks draped round their shoulders at rehearsal I realized that if Bazaar clothes were to be shown at all, they would have to be shown all together, one quickly following the other in the style of showing I liked.

Seen individually between two ball gowns, and dwarfed by the unbelievable splendour of the Palace ballroom with its opulent renaissance panelling, the very short flannel dresses with pleats above the knees that I had made, worn with coloured stockings and boots, would be nothing. The only possible way was to break the tempo of the whole evening with one great burst of jazz and let the girls come in at terrific speed in the zany, crazy way in which my clothes should be shown.

David was marvellous about it. I think he could see that the whole thing was showing signs of developing into something rather pompous and not the fun it was meant to be.

The girls backed me up marvellously. We had all become friends and they understood my clothes and what I was trying to do. The great difficulty was that the dressing rooms were miles away from the ballroom down long corridors. This could be overcome when the great ball gowns were being paraded because the girls had to walk slowly and this gave the next model time to catch up. But with the speed and impact I wanted, it was impossible.

The girls were splendid. Together we worked out that the only possible thing was to keep the Bazaar clothes just outside the ballroom in the corridor. We practised and experimented and rehearsed to find out just how quickly we could do this thing ... whipping off one thing in the corridor, leaping into the next, whizzing on. Together we managed to talk David round to our way of thinking. The Palace Hotel had never seen anything like it before.

The models were to make their entrance from a gallery above the ballroom and walk down the sweeping staircase. It was a very grand entrance. It was as if they were walking down from the dress circle into the orchestra stalls.

Bronwen Pugh opened the show. She was wearing a white lace trouser suit of mine with a tremendous white fur hat. She looked like Garbo. But Bronwen never took modelling too seriously. At heart she is a great comedienne. She can clown. And she has a terrific sense of timing.

At the top of the stairs she took up a tremendous stance. She stood motionless for a few moments; then, with a magnificent gesture, she kicked up one leg and ran down the stairs in a sort of Charleston manner. She was fantastic. She was a sensation. It was all so entirely unexpected. Everybody in the room had been looking politely bored. Suddenly everything was changed. The whole atmosphere was electrified. There was a stunned silence. Everyone stopped eating and drinking and talking.

The thing was that they were expecting to see nothing but the grand clothes of the haute couture. They had already seen and possessed plenty of them. They had several minks of their own in their wardrobes. I am sure they felt there was nothing new in fashion for them to see.

Bronwen caught their imagination and set the mood for the rest of the evening. When the time arrived for showing all the other Bazaar models one after the other at full speed, the orchestra had caught the feeling. The music changed to hot jazz. The girls pranced down the stairs, one after the other, wearing little high-waisted flannel dresses with white stockings, or alternatively, flannel tunics over red sweaters with red stockings to match. Nobody in the audience had ever seen this sort of thing before. It was a riot.

To finish our part of the show Bronwen appeared again, this time in an enormous white fox cossack hat and a white leather coat lined with white fox fur. She had knee high white leather boots. With a haughty gesture, she threw off her coat and threw back her head. In the panicky speed changes, she had forgotten to put on a dress!

One way and another the show was a success.

The grandees and the millionaires wanted these clothes. They had everything else; all the minks and ball gowns they could use; the silk shirts and the silk trousers; the stretch pants and the leopard tops. But they hadn't any fun clothes. This was something quite new to them and I had no idea to what extent this look was to grip people's imagination and how popular it was to become.

Like all women, these pampered people, in spite of their worldly sophistication and possessions, want to look as young as they possibly can and, in a way, this was the beginning of something we take almost for granted now ... grown-ups wearing teenage fashions and looking like precocious little girls.

We were told by the manager of the hotel that normally, after a show of this kind, all the guests disappeared. This did not happen that night. We were all asked to have dinner. The orchestra started playing something approaching jazz and soon we were all on the floor dancing. No one thought of going to bed or leaving the ball-room for the usual round of the village night haunts that evening. The whole place was alight until four-thirty in the morning.

When I finally got to bed I knew I was finished. On top of the flu which had been steadily piling up, all the strain and excitement of the show had been too much for me. I can hold off almost anything until a show is over; then I crumble. I knew I would not be able to go back to England with the others. They left the next day taking most of the clothes but leaving behind all the last minute things I had brought over with my personal luggage.

It was one of those mad things that seem to happen in my life. Here I was in one of the most luxurious hotels in the world with the largest possible number of clothes and practically no money.

All the boutiques in St Moritz wanted to buy the things I had shown and several of the people staying in the hotel wanted them too but of course I couldn't sell a thing as they were either 'in bond' or Bazaar models and I had to take them all back to England.

I spent a couple of days in bed. Then I felt fine. I began to enjoy myself. I had so many clothes to wear; so many different coloured stockings. These were sensational at the ski dances around five o'clock in the evening when everyone else was in ski trousers or silk pants.

I was dancing with an American and having such a marvellous time, particularly after feeling so rotten with flu, that I felt I wanted it to go on for ever. Just because of this feeling, I said to the drummer in the band as we were dancing by, 'How much longer? What time do you finish?'

I suppose I should have known better. The boy was an Italian ... very young ... very gawky ... with a mass of fair curly hair which made him look so like Harpo Marx that I couldn't help smiling. I was grinning all the time anyway because I was so happy to be well again and having such a wonderful evening. I found out, too late, that he completely misunderstood my smile ... and the meaning of my words. When the ski dance ended, I went out with the American friends I had made and they took me to all the little village bistros. We danced all night. It was five o'clock in the morning when we got back to the Palace. One of the Americans picked up my boots to carry them to my room.

I opened the door, turned on the light, and there – in the bed – was a sleeping figure. All we could see was a mass of curly fair hair on the pillows.

'They must have thought I had gone back to England. They have let my room. Whatever am I going to do?'

Then I realized that the floor was still covered with my cardboard boxes; I could see the white fox furs spilling out of the bulging wardrobe. I couldn't think what could have happened. We clambered over the boxes to the bed. The curly head never stirred. When I could see the face, I discovered it was the little drummer from the band. He was so fast asleep that we had to shake him to wake him up. When he did open his eyes, he was absolutely petrified. He leapt out of bed. He was in his pants. He started to cry. And cry as only an Italian can. He was pathetically young. He wouldn't stop crying and as he spoke very little English, we couldn't make him understand a thing. It was only after a tremendous effort that we found out the real cause of the tears. The fact was that he had no right to be in the hotel at all at that hour and if it were discovered, he would be sacked. It was nearer six o'clock than five by this time and already some of the staff were about. The thing was, how were we to get him out of the hotel without his being seen. He had only his band's uniform with him and he was bound to be spotted by the early morning cleaners and the night porters.

He had such a pretty baby face and he was so pathetically upset that suddenly I had an idea. He would look marvellous in a woman's clothes. We dressed him up in my things. We made him wear the white leather coat with all the white fox fur coming up high around his face. I put some make-up on him, added a dash of lipstick, then, as a final touch, put a huge white fur hat on top of his curls. He really looked rather gorgeous. Then the American took his arm and walked him out of the hotel.

Later we bundled up his uniform into a parcel and it was arranged that when it was all right for him to be seen about the hotel, he would come to my room, collect his things and leave the clothes he had borrowed in their place. How we ever managed to get him to understand all this I shall never know. But it worked.

Next day I went home. I had learned the enormous show-biz value of this kind of fashion show operation and I was full of ideas for expanding in London. I found Alexander and Archie in exactly the same frame of mind.

We all knew we had to open another Bazaar and we felt that somewhere in Knightsbridge would be right for us.

There was a new building going up opposite the tube station but it was desperately expensive. We thought it was a dream that could never be reality but we started discussing all sorts of possibilities all the same.

We thought of forming a joint company with Terence Conran (now of Habitat fame) and his first wife, Shirley, the Woman's Page feature writer on the *Daily Mail*. They would produce the fabrics; we would make the clothes. The five of us ... Terence and Shirley, Alexander, Archie and I – had endless lunches at Alexander's discussing what came to be known as Plunket's Proposition and one day Shirley came rushing in rather late with the news that there was a shop going in Knightsbridge and she had heard the rent might not be quite so high as we expected.

The thing was that there was some sort of temporary depression … the Bank Rate had gone up again or something like that. There was a fresh slump that lasted about four weeks and during that time all the Big Boys were frightened of doing anything new. While they were sitting tight to see which way the cat would jump, we took the plunge. We signed the lease. It was a huge shell of a shop. We were terrified. The rent was fantastic to us.

For some reason which I can't remember now we did it on our own. Terence designed the shop for us and we all plunged into the excitement of planning the fittings and decor for the Knightsbridge Bazaar. Then came the reaction … when we had to stand by watching the workmen get on with the job whilst all our money simply poured away at the most colossal rate.

We were so involved that, paradoxically, Alexander says he felt that at last he was in a position of power. He insisted that it was time we got married. He went ahead and made all the arrangements and forced it through.

We had often talked of marriage when someone else brought up the subject but somehow or other time passed and neither one of us was too concerned. The thing was that we had grown up together from such an early age; we had gone through everything together; it all seemed so completely right from the beginning that we just had not got round to the actual ceremony.

Our marriage has always been a happy and riotous one. We have always had a pretty good relationship. We don't bottle up our 'beefs'. They come out with a shout of rage and are forgotten. We would both like to have children; that's why Alexander insisted we must get married; but we are running so hard to keep up with ourselves there just has not been time so far. To haul off and take a year or however long it takes to have a baby is impossible when one has to design twenty-two collections a year. We have become involved in an industry. People – and their jobs – depend on us. Sometimes I think we could not possibly go on as we do if we did not enjoy each other so much. We are not alone. We are together in everything.

When we had actually fixed the date for our wedding, we suddenly became embarrassed about the whole thing. For ages afterwards we were so shy about it that we went on pretending we were 'living together'. It often happened that people would work for us for six months or longer without knowing that I was really Mary Plunket Greene. It took Ann Cossins who runs Chelsea Bazaar a year to catch on.

The first time we asked Ann to come home with us and have a drink I was so tired when we got there that I went into the bedroom, took off the dress I had been wearing all day and came back into the living-room in a dressing-gown. Poor Annie! She sat there getting more and more embarrassed and shocked at this open display of living in sin.

When she was told by one of the other girls that we had then been married for more than a year, she wouldn't believe it.

'They can't be!' she said. 'Not the way they behave!'

But we did in fact get married one day at Chelsea Registry Office. We kept the whole thing dark. We were terrified some of our friends might hear of it and turn up. We didn't tell one of them. My mother and father and Alexander's mother were the only witnesses. So far as everyone else was concerned, we decided it would be much more fun to let them go on believing we were living together.

We had an awful wedding. The Registrar, or whoever it was, put on a sanctified Dearly Beloved voice; he treated us in an impossibly pompous manner and went purple in the face with the effort.

Alexander gave me a wide plain gold ring, just the sort of big, positive ring I love. It was too large for my fourth finger so I started wearing it on my middle one and won't be parted from it long enough to have it altered. He had had a bit of luck playing Spoof so we were able to go off on a honeymoon. We went to Ibiza because I love the sun. Alexander hates it. It was the strangest honeymoon. He stayed in bed all day to keep out of the sun and I lay on the beach soaking it up.

We met up with two strange Americans ... a jazz musician and his girl friend. They had already been in Ibiza for several months and, like Alexander, looked as if they had never seen the sun. They stayed in bed all day, too. I was the only one trying to lead a double life – day and night. I bought a local bathing suit ... bright green wool with singlet type shoulder straps and four-inch legs. It looked great and I became addicted to wearing this. This bathing suit, dated, I suppose, about 1933, gave me ideas for a series of pinafore or jumper dresses which became a craze here and in America.

We had a splendid time with the two Americans. They knew all the night spots and we started to go around with them. The man played terrific jazz which endeared him to Alexander right away. We used to drink a mad Spanish brandy, made in one of the villages next door, which is as poisonous as it is cheap and, on this, we would get more and more sentimental as the night wore on.

There was one evening when we really did the town. We went to every night spot in the place. Alexander was wearing one of his silk suits. He has very positive ideas about how a man ought to dress and he had some new suits ... really rather flashy ... for our honeymoon.

Whenever we go on holiday he always takes silk suits and lawn shirts and sits under an umbrella. He thinks he looks terrible in sports clothes, which he calls 'separates'. In London he goes around in the most unbusinesslike suits but he is always dead dapper by the sea.

This particular evening we ended up in the early hours sitting outside a café on the front, watching for the dawn. We had been drinking masses of this cheap Spanish brandy. We were still drinking it. For some reason we were all nostalgic. We dug up all sorts of memories from our early lives. Alexander started talking about the Chaplin films ... the ones which always ended with the hero walking off alone into the sunset or into the dawn. It didn't matter whether it was a sad film or a happy one ... the solitary figure walking into the horizon brought a lump to the throat and often tears to the eyes too. Alexander said how true of life this was. This was how life was meant to end.

Suddenly the dawn broke. The sun switched on. It was all too much for us after all that brandy.

'How marvellous everything is,' Alexander said, tears pouring down his face. … 'I like my wife … she's the girl I always wanted. We have had a tremendous time with you two … you are a great jazz musician and you've got a frightfully pretty girl. We have enough money. It is so warm and lovely. This is the end as I want it to be.'

With that he got up from the table and walked slowly into the sea along the path of the rising sun. He did not take his clothes off. Neither did he swim. He just walked and walked and walked. Slowly the water came up higher and higher until the whole of his beautiful silk suit submerged and we could just see his head. And still he walked on … further and further away from the shore into that path of light.

And the three of us just sat there, doing absolutely nothing, smiling at each other like Cheshire cats … all feeling terribly sentimental and very near to tears but doing nothing about it. It must have been that poisonous brandy. I was told, later, that I sat there mumbling, 'He's right. Of course he's right. Pity. He was such a nice fellow.'

Instead of rushing round yelling, 'Save him! Save him!' we discussed seriously whether we should go in after him and do the same thing. Then suddenly we realized that we could not see Alexander. He had completely disappeared.

I did jump up then and start running about and yelling, wholly ineffectually. Nobody took the slightest notice of me. The Americans said we ought to have something to eat. We went back into the café and ordered coffee.

I was beginning to register and realize what had happened when Alexander walked in. Fortunately, when the water had gone right over his head and completely submerged him, he had sobered up with a bang. He started to swim. His sense of direction was not very good and he had come ashore about half a mile further down the coast. He was still wearing his elegant silk suit which was steaming in the heat of the early morning sun. He never wore it again.

We had been layabouts long enough. It was time to go home.

If the sun had done nothing else for me, it had cleared my mind. I knew now exactly what fashion meant to me and what I wanted to do when we opened in Knightsbridge.

Fashion is the product of a thousand and one different things. It is a whole host of elusive ideas, influences, cross-currents and economic factors, captured into a shape and dominated by two things ... impact on others, fun for oneself. It is unpredictable, indefinable. It is successful only when a woman gets a kick out of what she is wearing; when she feels marvellous and looks marvellous.

All women, whether they go to work on a bus or in a Bentley (and about eight million women in this country do go out to work) worry about what to wear. Dressing to go with the job and fit in with the sort of life a woman leads has always been a problem.

Dr Ernest Dichter, who is the President of the Institute of Motivational Research in New York, says that fashion does not just mean to be sexually attractive to the other sex, however important this may be. Fashion is a tool of competition in the sexual sense but it is also a tool to compete in life outside the home. People like you better, without knowing why, because people always react well to a person they like the look of. It is an integral part of taking a job. The modern girl is much more feminine than we imagine her to be.

To me a fashionable woman is one who is ahead of the current rage. She must have a personal style, be aware of it and wear those clothes that emphasize it. A fashionable woman wears clothes; the clothes don't wear her. Clothes are tremendously important. A woman knows instinctively if she is wearing the right thing. If she is, she immediately becomes more poised, more confident, more in control of any situation.

Clothes should live, breathe and move with the wearer.

I hope I never lose track of their purpose ... to dress a woman and make her look her best. There is nothing so extravagant as buying something that no one notices. I am absolutely against what I call negative clothes … the sort that do nothing, seem nothing and sometimes cost a lot of money.

Fashion should be important to a woman. If she thinks about the appearance of her house, her husband's car, her friends, the theatre, then she must think about her clothes.

The 'intellectual' girl who completely disregards fashion is not necessarily 'a square' but she has only limited intelligence. The old idea that a woman is either sexually attractive and destined for motherhood *or* an intellectual, has gone. A blue-stocking attitude – if such a thing is possible these days – is the pitfall of the young intellectual who does not realize that the clothes she wears express her personality and that many people will judge her on these externals only. She has got to learn that fashion is not frivolous; it is a part of being alive today.

'A square' – who is by no means always an intellectual – also is one who cannot be bothered to keep up with the changing trends of fashion. She is a little low on nerve. She is utterly resigned to never being right in fashion at the right moment; she would rather like to be but she is always finding out that just as she had got to like some feckless innovation, it is suddenly older than time.

The square has just about got used to wearing her sweaters nice and straight with a big, warm turtle collar, when the relentless edict goes forth that anything in the sweater line that is not desperately long is old-fashioned and is henceforth as dated as last year's Christmas card. She isn't really surprised, poor girl. She knew it would happen. It was the same with black leather coats and black stockings and those odd colours plum and ginger and the deeply V'd sweaters.

The square usually loves buying clothes but although she always means to buy something terrifically up to date, she nearly always ends up with something cool and classic and rather pretty. She may try on a white lace trouser suit with bell bottoms but she would be quite overwhelmed at the thought of walking into a room wearing it. Usually she buys another little black number instead.

She never quite knows what to do with costume jewellery and little scarves though she's quite sure she ought to buy them. She thinks her friends look awfully dashing in their patterned stockings and shiny white boots but only dares to wear them the year they go out of fashion.

She has been going to the same hairdresser for years and he does it very nicely. It's much the same year after year but people seem to think it suits her so why should she change? She has not the slightest idea what the word 'gear' means outside a car.

Curiously, quite a number of the women who are awarded the annual title of 'one of the world's best dressed women' are square. At any party the most elegant there may well be 'square'. But the most exciting will be Mods.

The square will be wearing something useful, slim, simple, pretty, probably beautifully cut and practically dateless. Inevitably it will be in a pretty colour and she will look essentially feminine – if you notice!

The girl who is with-it recognizes at once the difference between the 'intellectual' and the 'square'. She is observant and she likes being observed. She enjoys being noticed – but wittily. She is lively … positive … opinionated.

Women have denied for years that they choose clothes with an eye to man appeal. I think – and I am sure all switched on girls will agree with me – that sex appeal has absolutely Number One priority.

Personality counts later. So, of course, does an intelligent brain. But if you do not catch a man's eye in the first place you are never going to have the chance of showing him what a very nice dish you are.

A soft skin … skin that looks like skin and not a mask … is always an asset. So is hair that looks like hair. Hair has enormous sex appeal when it is patently clean and well brushed and shining. I have never been able to bear the look of lacquered hair.

I think there are two ways of looking appealingly sexy. There is the tough way (remember the blonde heroine dressed in men's clothing in the early American films?) and the pretty, feminine way which, strangely, often has the most effect when worn by a strong featured, boyish-looking girl, for example Romy Sneider. Every girl has to settle for herself on the style it is to be for her …

Back in London after our honeymoon, I started agonizing over the clothes I wanted to design for the collection with which we would open Knightsbridge Bazaar. Time flew. The day came. The new Bazaar was opened to the public.

The day after, Clare Rendlesham walked in. Perhaps 'walked' is the wrong word. Clare doesn't walk!

Clare stormed in. She marched round the shop, looking at everything. Then she turned on me. 'What do you mean opening a shop like this and not telling me about it? How could you do such a thing! Have any of the fashion girls seen these clothes?'

Clare at that time was working on *Vogue*. Pat Cunningham (Charles Creed's wife) was the fashion editor but Clare used to rush around and find out everything that was new. I believe she really started the 'Young Idea' feature in *Vogue* which became such a successful permanent feature.

Clare hardly gave us time to get a word in that day. At last we did manage to tell her that we would like to give a Press party very much indeed but we did not really know the right people to ask. Clare helped us. She really got us organized. She turned out to be a wonderful ally. She loves to help people.

She hadn't a great deal of power then – not nearly so much as she has now – but she has always had enormous talent. She picked up the subtle new feeling in fashion far more quickly than any other journalist. She had all the things I had not got and wished I had … personality and self-confidence, natural chic and incredible drive.

Alexander had some wild ideas for our first real Press party. We were determined it would be really something. We sent invitations to all the right people, guided by Clare, but a lot of them didn't turn up. They sent an assistant or a junior. We were far too unimportant then to be noticed officially by the fashion grandees.

We managed to persuade nine of the top photographic girls to model the clothes for us. We did this because I wanted to show the clothes moving, not parading, and these girls move beautifully and naturally. They walk swingingly and when they are still for a moment, they stand arrogantly. They absolutely bewitch me.

There are stairs at the back of the shop leading up to a small sort of gallery room. The models dressed up here and as they danced ... literally danced ... down the open stairway, a wind machine caught their skirts and blew them this way and that to create an even greater sense of speed and movement. This was really a development of all I had learned at the Palace Hotel in St Moritz. We had the right jazz music specially taped so there would be no gap in the music and these girls each stood, in turn, at the top of the stairs, then, with some terrific gesture, moved and danced down into the showroom.

We showed forty garments in fourteen minutes and every single minute was packed with incident. The girls just threw themselves into the spirit of the whole thing and acted like mad.

We were showing knee-high cowboy boots worn with fantastically short skirts; high-waisted tweed tunic suits with tweed knickerbockers; Norfolk jackets trimmed lavishly with fox collars. Eyebrows went right up to the hairline when the first model appeared.

One girl carried an enormous shotgun; another swung a dead pheasant triumphantly round her head. Perhaps too triumphantly because the poor thing, which we had bought from Harrods across the road, thawed out in the heat of the place and blood began spurting out all over the newly painted walls; even over some of the journalists.

Then we showed party dresses. The girls came whizzing down the stairs, an outsize glass of champagne in one hand, and floated round as if they had been to the wildest party or looking dreamily intellectual with a copy of Karl Marx or Engels in the other hand.

No one had seen anything like this before. No one had ever before used this style of showing in London or anywhere else. People were heard to say, 'The Method School of Modelling has arrived' and things like 'This is the wackiest show ever ... and the funniest!'

At the end, the place just exploded!

It was the most important thing that had ever happened to me. I was overcome by it all. Unaccountably, such sudden apparent success filled me with absolute horror. I was completely terrified of all the important people who now wanted to talk to me. I fled up the stairs with Clare behind me. I remember her shouting, 'Idiot! Why isn't Iris here? And Ernestine? We have got to do something about it!' I could not do anything about anybody at that moment.

Fortunately Clare took over. It is this enormous energy of hers; she is like a tornado. She adopted us. She was determined that we should meet all the top fashion writers. She kept on saying, 'No one has ever shown clothes in this way before. It is revolutionary. We must let everyone know about it.' The next day she brought Iris Ashley in to see us, and, soon afterwards, Iris gave us our first full page editorial in the *Daily Mail*.

Alexander says that it was Clare Rendlesham who inspired us; Iris Ashley who made us known to the masses; and Ernestine Carter who gave us the accolade of respectability.

It took Ernestine a little while to accept us wholeheartedly. I don't think she really approved of us at first. Perhaps she thought of us as degenerate. She did comment on us in the *Sunday Times* but we thought the remarks she made were rather snide. Eventually Alexander wrote to her and said how flattered we were that she should mention us at all but we did sometimes wonder whether perhaps she had got the wrong impression of what we were trying to do. He told her how much we would like to meet her personally and show her our clothes.

We had a friendly reply to this letter and she came along to Knightsbridge Bazaar to see what we were doing. The following Sunday she gave us a whole page in the *Sunday Times*. And for the next few years a whole series of pages punctuated by small pieces and pictures of our latest stuff. Goodness, how she helped us! Her interest in us culminated in the *Sunday Times* Award which was given to me for 'jolting England out of its conventional attitude towards clothes'.

But no one did more for us than Clare. She introduced us to everybody. She literally made people help us. She gave endless dinner parties for us. She would shake people and say, 'You have got to help these two.'

We started going everywhere together ... Clare and her husband, Tony Rendlesham, Alexander and I. We spent half our lives together. People became so accustomed to the sight of us together that we were invited everywhere as a foursome.

Clare bewitched and stimulated me. We discussed fashion endlessly. In some way she set off my ideas; I used to thrash them out with her, plotting and planning. She knew how to push in the right direction ... something Alexander and I have never really mastered. She is tremendously chic ... a fabulous woman.

Alexander is – and always has been – half in love with her but, for me, it is a love-hate relationship. Alexander knows how to treat Clare. I don't. I respect her enormously but sometimes I hate her at the same time. At first she frightened me. She is terribly grand and terribly rich and has the most terrific house in London and the sort of house I have always wanted in the country ... a whole row of old cottages reconstructed into the most super place.

Clare knew I was intimidated and enjoyed it. She never lets up. She is permanently on a starvation diet and makes everyone else feel positively fat. I know her tactics now. Before she throws a dinner party, she will starve for four or five days so that she can put on a good act of having a hearty appetite and eating well and so encourage all her women guests to let themselves go on the absolutely delicious food she produces. She knows I get the message now and we battle jokingly as to who can eat the least.

All the same I was terribly upset when, largely inspired by Clare, Woollands opened their 21 Shop. She organized their first Press party which was done on much the same lines as our opening of Knightsbridge Bazaar but with all the money in the world and therefore on a much grander scale. The whole thing was exaggerated in my own mind out of all proportion and this was helped, no doubt, by the fact that the overwork and strain and terror and excitement about all the publicity we were having, and all the unexpected success the Knightsbridge Bazaar had brought us, were beginning to come to a head.

The emotional strain was such that Alexander and I were both so overwrought that we were, for the first time, finding it difficult to live with each other. If you are married to the person you work with and you work together at such a high pitch and you both care about it all so much that you carry it on far into the night, there is no switching off. Our private lives had been taken over by the business. Wherever we were, whoever we were with, the conversation revolved round one subject – fashion.

All this boiled over when Susie died. I can hardly talk of Susie even now. Susie Leggatt was one of the first people we ever employed. She was one of the most beautiful girls I have ever seen: she had 'the Look' ten years ahead of her time; she had a terrific influence on me.

Susie first joined us at Chelsea Bazaar at a time when we were – as usual – short of money. We were terribly involved with plans for the opening of the Knightsbridge shop at the time and we needed someone to look after King's Road for us specially as I wanted to spend most of my time in the workrooms. Susie came in to see us with a friend of ours, Peter Sterry. She wasn't looking for a job … she was, in fact, a deb and a cracking snob! She just thought it might be rather jolly to work for a couple of weeks. As it turned out, she enjoyed it all so much and we became such friends that she was with us for nearly three years.

Susie was a neurotic … always handing in her resignation and prancing out; she had one hopeless love affair after another and at these times would create the most ghastly scenes.

But she was so wonderful looking and so much a part of the look I was trying to create that she contributed endlessly to the building of the character of Bazaar. She just seized on the ideas I was producing and knew immediately how to wear them. She had the look and the style and the arrogance that fitted in exactly with my clothes.

She was the first to wear black leather boots up to the knee (she wore them up to the crotch); the first to wear black stockings … black leather coats trimmed with black fox fur collars … and all the rest of it. To see the clothes I was making being worn by someone like Susie with such incredible panache gave me just the encouragement – and incentive – I needed.

Susie leapt on every new idea the instant I produced it. She had the nerve to wear it straight away. She looked so beautiful wearing 'the look' that other people were encouraged to try. Many people were frightened of my early designs but having once seen them worn by Susie, they were completely sold on the whole idea.

She seemed to know everybody in London. Friends of hers were constantly filling the shop … some of them chic and smart and beautiful; others the worst dregs of the rich social classes. She knew all the new young model girls, too, and they are always wonderful to dress.

When we opened Bazaar in Knightsbridge, Susie Leggatt took over and had six, sometimes eight, girls working with her, mostly debs and ex-debs like herself.

All these girls wore high black leather boots, black stockings and black leather coats. People began to queue to get into the shop just as they had done in the King's Road. The girls really put 'the look' across. They developed 'the cult', helped, to some extent, by a very enterprising young man, Andrew Oldham, who called himself my assistant cum window dresser cum everything else. Andrew can have been little more than sixteen at the time; he had just left school; but he had all the confidence in the world. Archie thought he was a very bright boy and did a lot to help him.

One day Andrew confided in Archie's wife, Cathy, that he could do any of our jobs standing on his head (Archie's included!).

Cathy asked him what he did. 'Well,' he said, 'when Mary's a bit tired, I design a few dresses for her; when Alexander is choosing stock, I chat up the Press for him. I could do it just as well on my own. It's easy!'

Then, suddenly, entirely unexpectedly, we got a note from Andrew on Bazaar writing paper. It was his formal resignation posted at the airport as he was leaving the country.

Archie heard of him a little later when he was apparently trying to get a job on *Time* magazine and the editor telephoned to find out whether anyone as young as Andrew could possibly have done all the things he claimed to have done. Nothing came of this but not long afterwards we heard that he had become manager of The Rolling Stones! Obviously, he was right in all that he claimed. Even at sixteen, he could have done any one of our jobs.

When Susie died very suddenly whilst she was on holiday in Tangier, I refused to believe it. I was heartbroken.

The business was expanding so rapidly. I had been working at such tremendous pitch all hours of the day and night. It was not that I felt we had taken on too much but that it seemed to be proving too much for me. I was so stewed up that I could not believe in the success everyone was claiming for me.

There is this awful thing when you have worked terribly hard for something and it comes off, there is an illogical, overwhelming anticlimax, a simply awful depression. I piled up in total depression. All I wanted to do was to lie on my bed staring at the ceiling with the tears running down my cheeks. I knew everyone in the firm was saying, 'Poor Mary! It's overwork!' Finally Alexander decided I simply had to have a holiday and get away from it all. It was at a time when we could not both be away from the business at the same time. It was November and he decided the only place where I could be sure of finding the sun within reasonable distance was Malta.

I was put on the plane. The journey was awful. I found all the other passengers were the wives and families of men stationed out there. The babies cried continuously the whole way. Lunch was boiled fish and cabbage.

The day I arrived, it started to rain, and I was told that once it started, it rained solidly throughout the month of November. It poured down at such a pace that it was impossible even to walk across the road; you had to find a taxi to take you.

Alexander had booked me into the largest and most awful hotel there … right in the middle of the barrack square. I was never allowed to forget it. There was the ceremony of hoisting the flag at daybreak and the ceremony of hauling it down again at sundown. There were parades. And there was non-stop military music all the time.

I found a tiny wireless in my room but the only thing I could get on it was the music relayed for the forces ... those extraordinary tunes the forces are supposed to want, interlaced with homesick messages for Mum. I could not bear it. It all made me want to cry more than ever.

So far as I was able to discover during the short time I stayed, every room in the hotel was painted either dark brown or navy blue. And the menu in the dining-room never changed ... fish and chips.

I tried to throw off my dreadful lethargy and depression by going into the bar for a drink. The whole place was electrified when I walked in. Apparently no single bird had ever been seen in the bar before. The women glared at me. The men tried to pick me up. It was quite obvious that everyone was thinking, 'What the hell is she doing in a place like this?'

I know I looked pretty extraordinary. I was wearing very short skirts and this was before short skirts had really been accepted in London – let alone Malta.

I went back to my room and this terrible music just went on and on. There wasn't a break in the clouds; it looked as if it would rain for ever. There was nothing for me to do but cry. There was that awful brown paint! I simply could not stand it. I rang the airport to find out when a plane was leaving. I was told the plane I had arrived in was taking off the next day. I took it. I didn't really know what I was going to do although I was determined that I was not going straight back to London. The trouble was that I had very little money. I had never been abroad on my own before and my plane ticket and the hotel expenses and everything else that could be foreseen had been booked and paid for in London before I left. Fortunately I found out at the airport that I could trade in my return ticket for a leap-frog ticket. This would give me the right to get off the plane anywhere en route.

I left Malta in the plane I had arrived in. We touched down first at Naples. I realized that I had practically no money for food. I would have to be terribly careful.

I decided that the best thing for me to do would be to get on a plane at least once a day and, in this way, I would be able to have one meal a day at the expense of the aircraft company. When I booked a seat, I made a point of inquiring whether or not meals were served on the flight. One day I found I was eating lunch in the air about half-past eleven in the morning; the next day my first meal would be dinner on another plane at about half-past six in the evening. Travelling in this way I managed to visit most of the European airports. But it was a hopeless way to try to live.

When I reached Rome, I simply could not go on any longer with this nomad existence. I was no longer on the verge of tears; I cried all the time quite shamelessly. And it was still pouring with rain. Wherever I went, I could not get away from the awful rain. And, in Rome, it was freezing!

I walked out of Rome airport feeling suicidal. Down the road I came upon a small hotel. It appeared to be made of marble. It was spotlessly clean. I booked in. Bed and breakfast only. I could not afford anything more. I had to stay put for a few days. I could not face another plane. When I got to my room, I found they had given me a wonderful private bathroom. This probably saved me. When I was not actually sleeping, I spent the next four days lying in the bath.

Fortunately I had with me a huge supply of paperback tragedies ... Russian ones. Lying in the bath, I read every one of these from cover to cover. I managed to fix the taps so that I could have a trickle of hot water running all the time and adjusted the plug so that just the right amount of water ran away. I never left my room. All I had to eat was the breakfast the waiter brought in in the mornings.

Obviously the hot baths were a terribly good idea. I was told afterwards that even lunatics respond to this sort of treatment. One morning I woke up and I knew I was cured. Suddenly I felt on top of the world again. I was able to cope with anything. Every bit of the depression had gone.

I went right out of the hotel and walked back to the airport. I wanted to get home but I had to time my plane so that I would be sure of getting a good meal. I was terribly hungry.

It just happened that the man behind the desk doing the bookings that day was sympathetic. I found myself explaining to him just how important it was for me to travel in a plane which served food. He promptly insisted on taking me out to dinner that night. This meant I had to stay another night in the hotel but with the prospect of a good meal ahead, I could face it.

That evening we went in his car up into the mountains to the villages that overlook the city. There are marvellous little restaurants there which are the centre of all village life. Fires blaze on the hearth and all the local families come in … the children, the grandparents, the lot … They sit round long trestle tables. Everybody knows everybody else. The food is put in enormous dishes right down the centre of these tables … absolutely terrific food. There were no tourists there. It was completely out of season. This was a marvellous night for me. It was my first real meal for a week. I ate more than I had ever eaten before. It was a riotous evening.

The next day, this man booked me on a plane which had a super reputation for superb food. The rain stopped. The sun came out. Everything in my world was wonderful again. We flew up the coast of Italy while I tucked into roast duck.

The plane was full of Americans; obviously they had heard of the reputation of this plane too. When we sighted Mont Blanc they all brought out their movie cameras and our pilot, who seemed determined to make sure that every one of his passengers had a marvellous time, circled the mountain twice so they could all get good shots of it to send back home. I like Alitalia.

When we arrived in Paris, I went straight to the hotel where Alexander and I always stay and where I knew I would be known and credit would not be too complicated to arrange. It was snowing and I looked ridiculous in the little cotton dress I was wearing (designed for the Maltese sun?) with everyone else huddled up in fur and boots. But I did not care. Nothing worried me. I was feeling marvellous.

The following morning I was back in London. I found everything at Bazaar booming. I thought that now – at last – I could accept the success that had come to us so suddenly and unexpectedly and enjoy it.

Alexander was so elated that I had come home so completely recovered and so soon that he decided the time had come for us to visit America. We went off with two suitcases full of designs, a couple of telephone numbers given to us by journalist friends, a lot of excitement and a great deal of apprehension.

We had done no market research on what we might expect to find over there. We had no influential contacts. We really did not mean to try to sell anything. We just thought we ought to know something of the way life went over there and have a look at the shops so that we might know the sort of thing the Americans liked. Nobody – not even us – thought my fashion thinking would ever have any influence outside London.

We went at practically a moment's notice and it was only twenty-four hours before we were due to leave that Alexander discovered that we had to produce photographs of ourselves for the visas. The shops where they do these things near the Embassy were closed but we were told that there was a machine ... a sort of do-it-yourself job ... that we could work ourselves somewhere in Bayswater. We eventually found it, a prehistoric, battered old thing that worked when half-a-crown was put in the slot. It was not in very good working order. The camera dragged our faces out so that we looked like a pair of disconsolate bloodhounds. Every feature was elongated. They are delirious pictures.

For two whole days after we got to New York we were too scared to make a telephone call. When we did get going, one of the first things to happen was very discouraging. We had been told that we must make ourselves known to a woman called Tobe, a great merchandising expert hired as an adviser by many of the big departmental stores. She also had a column in the New York *Herald Tribune* which was syndicated throughout the States. We were told she had enormous power.

We went to see her, taking the few things we had brought with us. We found a little, round frog sitting on an extraordinary great dais in the middle of a huge office, surrounded by countless specialized experts. There was a shoe editor ... scarf editor ... jewellery editor ... underwear editor ... handbag and glove editor ... and so on and on. She had somehow acquired the amazing power of a dictator. Manufacturers would go and show her what they were producing and if she liked the things, they were made. She would recommend them to the hundreds of stores who bought her services and she would write them up in her column.

Tobe did not like us one little bit. She looked at our stuff. Then she said one word, 'Crap!'

This should have been enough to send us dashing to the airport to catch the next plane back to London but somehow the whole setup was so phoney. Alexander refused to take her seriously. He was not in awe of her as I was. He whispered, 'She does not know what she is talking about!'

And the blow was softened a little when two or three of the young editors working with her followed us out of the office and said they simply loved the things we had shown ('they were just *darling*') and how sad they were that Miss Tobe didn't approve.

The next day Alexander went out and bought the New York *Herald Tribune* (which we had never seen before) so that we could read Tobe's column. Then we cared even less. It really was a load of rubbish. Things like … 'Tobe says white gloves are always lovely in the spring …' etc. etc.

We stopped worrying. In fact, the next day we forgot about Tobe altogether. We had shown the collection – if you could call the few things we had with us in those two suitcases a collection – to *Women's Wear Daily*, the most powerful fashion newspaper in the world and the bible of the American fashion industry. They were wonderful to us. They raved about what they called the new international fashion look. They said, 'These Britishers have a massive onslaught of talent, charm and mint-new ideas. English chic is fiercely NOW … by the young for the young … coky, not kooky. Where did the English chic come from? It has always been there but it's on an added fashion wavelength now. Where is English chic going? How high is the moon?'

We could not believe it. We read it over and over again. This really got us going in the States.

Sally Kirkland of *Life* magazine read what *Women's Wear Daily* had said and she phoned to say she would like to see our clothes. Rosemary McMurtry of *Seventeen* magazine was so enthused that she suggested a special promotion; Eugenia Shepard of the New York *Herald Tribune* sent an assistant to see us and we were written up on her pages. We lived in a whirl of excitement.

The day Sally Kirkland was coming to our hotel, we lunched with Edward Rayne. He was frightfully good to us and arranged for us to meet Gerry Stutz, Vice-President of Henry Bendell, a small but very go-ahead store in New York ... the chic-est. It was a very grand lunch ... one of our few grand occasions on that trip.

Gerry Stutz was nice to us and kind about the clothes. She said Bendells would like to buy a few of our things. It all seemed too marvellous for words. We never thought of the time. Suddenly we realized that we were going to be late for Sally. We had to get right across Manhattan. We could not find a taxi. We half ran, half walked. When we did finally spot a taxi, we flung ourselves inside. Then we found we were only about two hundred yards from our hotel. The driver was frightfully rude!

We dashed up to our room in an awful state then found all the fuss had been completely unnecessary. Sally turned up two hours late. People in the fashion business nearly always do. But she was worth waiting for. She is absolutely tremendous. To us, when she walked in, she seemed to be the complete American girl ... long, gangly legs and a hoarse gravelly voice. She is full of jokes; she is matey and witty and has the most scandalous stories about the fashion grandees. She seemed to go absolutely mad about the clothes and when she left, said, 'We'll do a story.'

This was the beginning of three nutty days. We spent the time dashing all over New York with Sally and her photographer. I must have changed my clothes, the models two sizes too big, at least ten times a day.

Sally's idea was to start off her feature with one terrific picture of Alexander and me running down Park Avenue with a giant sheepdog and follow this up with pictures of us taken in New York and London.

It took ages with the sheepdog to get the shot Sally wanted. We began to realize that a magazine like *Life* takes about ten times as much material as they are ever likely to use and that the three days they were spending with us to get one picture meant nothing at all to them.

To us, it was wild. From living in a small hotel and eating at lunch counters, we were transported into a world where everyone welcomed us because we were being photographed by *Life*. We were made to feel we owned New York. Everywhere we went we were given V.I.P. treatment; at the night clubs we sat in the grandest seats and were introduced to all the most amusing people; in the restaurants, we sat at the best table with the head waiter giving us his personal attention; in Harlem, Alexander was photographed playing with Dizzie Gillespie's band. Somewhere, in some musty old drawer in the *Life* offices, there must be a thousand pictures of us in every amusing place in town.

The whole thing avalanched. *Life* magazine had set its official seal on us. People began to talk about us; journalists came to interview us; the store buyers were anxious to see more of our designs. *Women's Wear Daily* kept on writing about us and there were terrific write-ups in lots of other papers as well. Everyone was incredibly generous to us.

Rosemary McMurtry, the fashion director of *Seventeen* magazine, planned a promotion she was going to do with our clothes for the spring. We knew this would be a colossal boost for us.

Seventeen is the biggest selling junior magazine throughout the States and they have an absolutely clear picture of their readers. They know exactly who they are going for, why they are going and what they are going to achieve. Commercially, *Seventeen* is phenomenal. I think *Seventeen* and the French magazine *Elle* are the two most professional magazines in the world. To think that *Seventeen* had chosen my clothes for a major spring promotion was something I could never even have dreamed of.

Rosemary said that she would be able to arrange for a manufacturer in New York to make up the clothes necessary to back the editorial pages she would be giving us and that she would get

Saks of Fifth Avenue to stock them. She wanted me to design a new group of summer sports clothes and beach clothes and the idea was that these should be photographed in London against obviously recognizable British backgrounds. We were to be paid hundreds of dollars for each design. This was wonderful. It did, in fact, more than pay all our expenses for the whole trip and we had been rather worried about how it was going to be paid for.

Alexander said that he thought we would have to start thinking about going into mass production. The trouble was that we hadn't the slightest idea how to do it. The important thing was to get home and re-think the whole thing. I knew that for a spring issue of *Seventeen*, the clothes would have to be ready to be photographed in London at the end of January at the latest. I started thinking continuously in terms of sports clothes. There was not any time to lose.

The influence of New York had been enormous. To me, the place is electric. The energy, the excitement, the professionalism; even now, when we are more or less transatlantic commuters, these things still stagger me.

The greatest thing that ever happened to me, professionally, was that first trip to the States. It changed my whole thinking. I had never before met women so professional in their approach to business who could work at the pitch they do. Maybe it is their climate, because while I am there I begin to get something of the same kind of feeling. It is like sitting on top of the Alps absolutely shot with adrenalin.

I had seen things I had never before seen in England ... revolutionary things like the incredibly accurate sizings they have. They seem to know how to mass produce for every possible female shape. I found that if a woman knew her size she could just walk into any shop and buy off the peg without trying on. The most she might have to do would be to turn up the hem or shorten the sleeves. Buying a new dress was as simple as walking into an electrical department to buy a new plug for a lamp standard. I knew this was something we really had not mastered in this country. I don't think we have completely mastered it yet ... it is something I am always beefing about.

Proportioning is desperately important to mass production. It is, in fact, the very crux of modern design. Why is it that in this country we consider proportioning and the grading of sizes a humble job to be given to the youngest newcomer on the staff? I have seen it so often. A bright young thing joins a mass production firm and the first thing she is told to do is to grade the sizes. However bright she may be, she simply has not got the knowledge to do this. She goes round the edges painstakingly, adding an inch all round in an utterly unrealistic way.

When you grade up a dress, you can't simply add an inch or two to the hem and an inch or two on all the seams. The scaling of the collar ... the positioning of the pocket ... the size of the cuffs ... the length and placing of the darts; all these – and every single other detail – has to be taken into consideration and adjusted.

It takes real originality and designing sense to do this. There is something almost sculptural about it ... it is a job for the expert, not the beginner, however gifted that beginner may appear to be.

I came back to London bewitched by the American coordinates too. Separates are the youngest, cheapest and easiest way of putting two and two together. I wanted to design complete ranges of separates, each garment designed to complement another, each part capable of interlocking one with the other to mix and match to such an extent that it would take a computer to work out all the possibilities.

Every girl should go for separates. She should think of each piece as part of a jigsaw, then build up a comprehensive fashion picture. I would suggest a wardrobe in miniature like this. Take a pinafore dress, a jacket, skirt, sweater, pants and shirt that all go happily together and you have umpteen outfits. You have a sleeveless dress, a dress and jacket, a suit, separate skirt and sweater or skirt and shirt or shirt worn over the sweater with the skirt and trouser suit. A girl would need only a topcoat to complete a host of different-looking all-occasion clothes. And there need be positively no colour problems. Everything should be checked or plain or spotted in colours that go together. Fashion should be a game and it is fun to work out for yourselves the different ways of wearing the different garments.

Co-ordinates are a godsend to the woman with sizing troubles. Not all bust sizes are in the exact proportion to hip measurement that manufacturers have decided to regard as normal. Not everyone is made to the exact pattern of a size 12 or 14 or 16. Anyone with such a problem can buy the top she wants in the size she is looking for, then pick from a multitude of skirts on the separates rails that go with the blouse. They are a godsend to the traveller, too. A silk shirt that is perfect with a suit by day is equally right teamed with a matching or contrast silk skirt for dinner at night. The girl on a budget has always been aware of their advantages; she knows that one good skirt will do duty with half a dozen different 'tops' for countless occasions.

I never make separates which have to be worn either morning, afternoon or evening. I think clothes should adapt themselves to the moment. Girls in their teens and twenties are busy people who have no time to switch clothes during the day. They want clothes they can put on first thing in the morning and feel right in at midnight; clothes that go happily to the office and equally happily out to dinner.

The one-occasion dress is the dearest in the long run.

In spite of what I have said here, I was not so bemused by America that I came home thinking everything there was in advance of what we had at home. The window displays in the stores there are not nearly as original as many I have seen in London and even in our provincial cities.

And there seemed to me to be a great lack of co-ordination between promotion and point of sale. I found that I could look through a copy of *Seventeen* or *Mademoiselle* or *Glamour* and see the most exciting-looking clothes but when I wanted to buy one of these, it was awfully difficult to find one in the shops. In some cases, you eventually find out after a long, fruitless search, that only one store in the city has bought one of the dresses and that is unlikely to be in the size you want.

The fact is that there is far more fashion being sold across this small country than in the States. A girl is far less likely to be disappointed when she is looking for a particular garment here than she is there.

London led the way in changing the focus of fashion from the Establishment to the young. As a country, we were aware of the great potential of this change long before the Americans or the French. We were one step ahead from the start; we are still one step ahead and we have simply got to stay that way.

New York fashion is established fashion ... poised, sophisticated, woman-of-thirty fashion. The birds there don't have the chance to originate their own ideas. They have to conform to the gimmicks and good times the Madison Avenue boys dream up.

I knew we had a great opportunity to show America what British fashion can produce when I got down to work on the things I wanted to design for *Seventeen*. Rosemary McMurtry wrote from New York that she was coming over in the New Year and bringing a photographer, Joe Santoro, with her. She was leaving it to us to find the right model girls and to choose the locations.

We found four terrific girls who were delighted at the prospect of four days' work at American model rates which are three or four times more than is normally paid here. But they had to suffer for their money, poor things. It snowed the whole time Rosemary was here and it was appallingly cold.

Fortunately Joe Santoro had masses and masses of different filters for his camera, some of them miraculously designed to make the dreariest day appear in the finished photograph as summer heat. The girls were marvellous about it all. It was ghastly for them posing in a minimum of clothing and trying to look as if they were basking in brilliant sunshine on a freezing day.

We had a fleet of cars, well heated, for them to change in and we kept them going on continuous cups of boiling hot coffee laced with brandy. Joe took photographs in the Mall, outside Buckingham Palace, with the Horse Guards, by the gates of Royal Hospital and even some bathing in the sea at Brighton. Somehow the girls managed to look terrific. The pictures all came out. Looking at them in *Seventeen* magazine three months later, you would have thought they had been taken early in the morning on a summer day. There was that sort of lovely haze you see when it's going to be really hot. Joe's filters had done the trick. They were great pictures. The girls looked absolutely relaxed and not one of the magazine's readers can have suspected that they were actually bright blue and covered with goose pimples.

The American manufacturer Rosemary had tied up to make up the clothes which were to be shown in the promotion for Saks sent his designer over to get things lined up. It was this girl, Erica Elias, who gave us our first insight into all the little things that are so important and have to be taken into consideration in mass production. Such things as 'are four buttons really necessary? Wouldn't three do just as well?'

I had never had to think about this sort of thing before but when you are planning garments to be made in thousands even something as insignificant as the number of buttons becomes of vital importance. The influence of this on me was stupendous. It was great experience (though, of course, I could not know this at the time) for what lay ahead.

Not long afterwards we had a telephone call that was to change the whole course of our business lives … to spark off an entirely new outlook on our business … to establish us in the fashion trade in America and in other parts of the world; and to mushroom, eventually, into a multi-million-dollar deal.

We got back to the office one afternoon to find a message that a Mr Paul Young had phoned to make an appointment to see the collection. The name 'Paul Young' meant nothing to us and we were in fact out when he arrived with a Mr Bob Pegna of Portman's. My assistant, Shirley Shurville, looked after them, showed our things and entertained the two men. Later she phoned us and said, 'We have had some people called Penney in; they want you to call them.'

Apart from the fact that Penney was a third new name to us, they had left a whole lot of conflicting phone numbers; the whole thing seemed very fishy to us. We rang one number and found it was an hotel but they had no record of a Mr Penney there (of course we should have asked for Mr Young). Then we rang the next number which we assumed was Portman's and found we were on to Selfridge's (we did not know that Portman's is the export division of Selfridge's). We could not understand it at all. We gave up.

Finally Paul Young came through to us and we arranged to meet. We all got on tremendously well from the start and I showed him the new clothes I was working on instead of those he had already seen hanging up in the stockroom. It turned out that he was the representative of the J. C. Penney company ... the biggest chain of stores throughout America.

James Cash Penney, the founder of these stores, is a most remarkable man. He and his wife opened one small shop in some small mining town in the Middle West back in 1901 on money borrowed from the bank. He is a staunch Baptist ... a very religious man ... and I imagine this was a pretty rare thing in those pioneering days. From the start his golden rule of trading has been complete honesty. Partly because of this he prospered and when his wife became pregnant he was able to take on an assistant. This young man worked hard and did well but, after a time, when the baby no longer needed her full-time attention, Mrs Penney found she was bored at home and longed to be back helping her husband in the store.

James Cash Penney didn't want to sack his young assistant. To keep his wife happy, he decided to buy another store fifty or sixty miles further down the track and put the assistant in charge there. He made it a fifty-fifty arrangement. He would finance the place; his assistant would work it; the profits would be shared between them.

This is the method he has adopted throughout all the stores – there are 1,700 of them now – which he subsequently opened throughout America. Even to this day, the manager of each one of them has a strong personal interest in success. I have been told that in some of the stores there are years when the manager earns more than the president of the company.

As the years of this century went by, people began to regard Penney's as so worthy and solid and trustworthy as to be dull and old-fashioned. Some of the old customers began looking to rival stores who appeared to be more tuned in to the post-war wavelength. Eventually the Penney managers got together and decided that some excitement was essential. They thought of a European promotion. They would get designs over from Britain, France and Italy and make a big thing of these in some of the stores.

Paul Young, a particularly bright young man, then in quite a junior position in the control buying office, was chosen to go to Europe for six months, look around and get ideas. He was given a pretty wide brief ... to bring back something good and exciting even if he might be doubtful about the selling possibilities of the merchandise. All he had to remember was that whatever he brought home must be unusual enough to cause comment and arouse interest and bring in the customers to look – if not to buy.

Before he arrived in London, Paul had visited France, Italy and the Scandinavian countries. He had seen some of the publicity we had had in the States in *Women's Wear Daily* and in *Life* magazine and he had made up his mind to have a look at what we were doing before he came to any final decision.

Penney's agents in London are Portman's and when Paul Young saw Bob Pegna there, he asked about us.

'Never heard of the name,' Bob Pegna said.

They looked us up in the phone book. The result was the mysterious phone call we got at the office.

When Paul saw the clothes I was working on, he got frightfully excited. He asked us if he could put a call through to New York. We heard him say on the phone, 'I have seen this person in Paris, that one in Italy, so-and-so in Spain. I have been to Denmark and Sweden and I have been to Ireland. There is nothing to touch Mary Quant. I absolutely believe that our whole project should be launched on this girl. Forget about the original idea of a European promotion.'

Of course we couldn't hear the reaction to all this at the New York end but obviously they accepted Paul's judgement. I was told to go ahead and design a small collection for the American market in junior sizes and intended, primarily, for teenagers. Paul said that

Penney's would probably take four collections a year and as a sign of good faith and proof of genuine interest, he placed an initial order for 6,235 garments, which seemed a hell of a lot in those days.

We were terribly anxious to sign the contract Penney's offered us. Financially it would go a long way towards putting us firmly on our feet. But with the methods of production we had then, it appeared to be completely beyond us.

That was the moment when Bob Pegna proved himself to be such a good friend. He controlled, through Portman's, all the export from this country to Penney's. From the moment we met, Bob treated us in an absolutely businesslike manner but he backed us all the way through. He got on with the organization of the whole thing and made it work.

When you think how amateur and ignorant we still were about the whole international business of fashion, this was quite something. I have always thought that Bob Pegna should be given a slice of the credit for the tremendous growth of international recognition of British fashion. It is no longer just us, but people like us, who are producing the biggest sellers in the American coast-to-coast catalogues, in the pattern books and even in some of the retail stores. We certainly could never have had the flying start in mass production which we achieved without the backing of his courage, enterprise and initiative.

He introduced us to Leon Rapkin of Steinberg's.

No designer, however talented, can be successful in a mass market without the wholehearted co-operation and backing of a manufacturer willing to meet him – or her – half-way.

Leon Rapkin and his firm did just this. They met us halfway. With brilliant insight and understanding, they seemed to sense from the start what could be done with the clothes I was producing ... and what could not be done, of course ... they gave us encouragement and practical help (we needed this badly). We kicked off in the most disastrous way with our first consignment. We were late with deliveries and we discovered, too late, that we had not been able to master American sizings. They taught us understanding of the peculiar problems of mass production methods; they gave us the knowledge and appreciation we now have of the teamwork that is an essential part of any successful venture of this kind.

I hope there are many British manufacturers who will be prepared to take the same chance with new young designers because this is the only way that Britain will keep the lead in this field we have managed to establish over the past few years.

World markets must be the aim of every British fashion designer today. If you specialize in beachwear, resort wear, ski wear ... in fact, if you make anything that women are happy to wear, you cannot risk focusing on the conservatively-minded minority. Style now has to be truly international ... to be as acceptable to the girl in Birmingham as it is in Bangkok ... to look as right on the girl in Boston as it does on the girl in Brighton.

What ready-to-wear does today, the couturiers – even the Paris couturiers – confirm tomorrow. It has happened several times already. I think it will go on happening.

Ready-to-wear designers and manufacturers have as much feeling for fashion's evolution – probably even more for day-to-day needs in clothing – as any Paris name. But there has got to be give and take on both sides. It must be a fifty-fifty understanding. The manufacturer has got to take a considered gamble ... the designer has got to learn to drop all sorts of things she wants and sacrifice all kinds of ideas simply because these are ideas which cannot be produced within the price range of a mass market.

Just as it is pointless to design a Rolls-Royce, then pare it down and down until it is supposed to fit into the mass market of the Mini Minor, so is it pointless in fashion to create a couture design and imagine it can be adequately produced cheaply in quantity.

You must know your medium from the beginning; from the first moment the designer's pencil goes on paper. Fashion must be created from the start for mass production with full knowledge of mass production methods. These methods must be exploited to the full and all the many talents that go to make up the industry co-ordinated and brought together. Fashion for the masses has got to be teamwork from start to finish. It cannot be a one-man band.

When, with the help of Steinberg's, we had the whole thing more or less under control, Alexander and I were invited to launch the American project from the British Embassy in Washington.

It was the first time ever that the clothes of a named British designer had been promoted throughout a large chain of stores across the States. It was exciting but worrying too. We thought perhaps that by linking the name of Mary Quant so closely with a chain of retail stores we might damage the image we were trying to create in the department stores. It seemed to us rather like trying to sell to Fortnum and Mason and Marks and Spencer at the same time. We had no idea what the reaction might be over there.

Our decision was finally influenced by our belief that the whole point of fashion is to make fashionable clothes available to everyone. Fashion is an inherent thing and should not be something which depends solely on beautiful and expensive cloth and hand work. It should be mass produced. I had a feeling that this was my opportunity to prove I really meant what I had so often said. Also the money was good. We decided to go ahead. We accepted Mr James Cash Penney's kind invitation.

John Cowan, the photographer who had taken the pictures in London for our first *Life* magazine feature, came down to the airport to see us off. It was only when we were saying goodbye to him that I discovered I had forgotten my passport. It was too awful. They said I could leave the country without it but I certainly would not be allowed to land on the other side. Alexander said I would have to risk it; we simply had to be in Washington the next day. Somehow we managed to get on the plane.

Soon after we were airborne, the Captain sent a message; 'What are you going to do? You won't be allowed to leave the airport. You will simply have to come straight back.'

Alexander had a brainwave. He asked the Captain to radio the Embassy. 'They are giving a huge party for us tomorrow and they will be almost as embarrassed as we if we don't turn up.'

Somehow or other the message was sent off. I doubt if it ever got through to the Ambassador himself but it certainly reached someone able and willing to help.

When we landed at Idlewild, the airport authorities had been contacted by the Embassy. They knew all about me. We were cleared and after we had gone through Immigration, we took off again, this time for Washington. We were treated like royalty. It was absolutely fantastic. Apart from this, it was the first time we had ever flown first-class and we were tucking into caviare and champagne all the time.

About twenty minutes before we were due to land, the Chief Steward came over to me with another message. 'We have received a radio from Washington,' he said. 'They have asked that you should be the first to step off the plane so that the television cameras and photographers can get pictures.'

This threw me into complete panic. I was so embarrassed I didn't know what to do. I sidled off to the lavatory to change my dress because I always travel in dowdy old gear. I locked myself in and started brushing my hair. I knew that it was going to be utterly impossible for me to walk down the gangway facing a barrage of photographers.

Poor Alexander! At first he sat there imagining I was spending a long time putting on lipstick and touching up my mascara. When the order came 'Fasten your seat belts … no more smoking' and I was still locked in the lavatory, he began to get worried. He banged on the door; the stewardess banged on the door.

I would not – could not – open it.

The plane landed, taxied to a halt and there, sure enough, was a massed bank of flash cameras, movie cameras, television cameras … the lot!

Quite obviously a tremendous publicity job had been done by the Embassy and by the Penney company. Looking at them all standing there I felt thoroughly idiotic. I could not face it. This kind of thing had never happened to me before; it might be great for a film star but for someone like me it was nonsense. I knew if I walked out I would fall flat on my face down the steps. I could not come up to scratch and do what was expected of me.

I could hear the other passengers in the plane getting more and more impatient at the delay. Alexander asked the chief steward to allow everyone else off the plane first. He still thought I might come to my senses and regain my confidence. But it was hopeless.

Finally, the cameramen got bored with waiting and no doubt cross. They packed up and disappeared. I watched them all go and it was only when the whole place appeared to be deserted that I came out. I crawled down the steps of the plane, very shamefaced, and carrying as many of our cardboard boxes as I could hold to hide as much of me as possible.

One of the J. C. Penney representatives was still waiting. He was pretty angry about the whole thing and terribly disappointed. He took a few half-hearted snaps with his Brownie and we were driven to a hotel near the Embassy. By this time I was feeling thoroughly doubtful about the success of the operation planned for the following day.

We found we had been given a smashing suite in the hotel and we had hardly put our things down when the telephone rang. Alexander answered. It was a woman.

'Hallo,' she said, 'how are you?'

Then she went on to proposition Alexander.

'Would you like to have a good time tonight?'

'What fun,' Alexander replied. 'Well, yes, that would be lovely. Who is it?'

'Oh, you won't know me but I would love to show you a good time.'

Alexander thought it must be someone from the Embassy and was very polite and enthusiastic but after a lot of mis-communication he twigged that this particular sort of good time would exclude me and he hung up rather red in the face.

The next morning we spent rehearsing at the Embassy. The show was to be put on in the Rotunda, an enormous great circular place where even the curtains were worked by electricity.

I had always thought of Embassies as rather stuffy places, terribly out of touch and out of date. How wrong I was! Here I found everyone tremendously switched on; completely with it and aware of the potential value of what we were trying to do. They wanted to build up exports from Britain just as much as we did in our private way and they were prepared to do everything possible to help.

The Rotunda was decorated with all those things which we in Britain tend to look upon as rather foolish ... Beefeaters, London policemen, pipers, red pillar boxes and all that rubbish. It all looked unmistakably British.

Ronald Arculus, the Commercial Attaché, had done a terrific job. He had made sure that all the important American fashion buyers would be there and all the Press. He had arranged for quite a number of them to fly in from New York, Chicago, Boston and so on.

After the rehearsal and before the show in the afternoon, James Cash Penney, described as 'the spryest granddaddy of American retailing' had decided to give a lunch party for all the grandees of the Embassy and of the American fashion world in one of the big Washington hotels. This was our first meeting with the great man. I suppose he must be in his eighties, probably his nineties. Whichever it may be, he is fantastic.

We saw him arrive, striding into the hotel in his king-size stetson with its plastic wrapper, surrounded by his heads of departments and looking just as if he had stepped right out of an early American Western ... except for the plastic hat wrapper! He had been up since before five that morning, had flown half-way across America and looked tremendous.

At this luncheon J. C. Penney sat at the top table with all his local store managers. Alexander and I sat at a table much lower down and, lower still, sat the First Secretaries and the buyers and the Press. According to our ideas of a promotion party over here, it was a crazy table arrangement. Thank God the Ambassador wasn't there!

No one had warned us that Baptists don't drink and don't approve of anyone else doing it either. And they don't smoke. Coffee was served continuously right through the meal and although we had by this time grown accustomed to drinking masses of coffee when in America, this was a bit much.

Then Mr Penney began to speak. He must have talked for a full twenty minutes ... all about how to live the pure life and end up ninety and hale and hearty and how to be a millionaire and things like that. Over here I am sure half of the guests would have walked out but in the States J.C.P. is a great figure. He is regarded as symbolic and a part of the great American tradition. Actually, it wasn't a bad speech once one got over the surprise.

We got some idea of the size of his empire when we asked Paul Young if he had personally visited all the stores and he said, 'No. Covering one a day, it would take me about six and a half years!'

The show in the Rotunda was a huge success. About sixteen of my designs (those picked out for intensive promotional backing) were shown.

Lady Ormsby-Gore came and sat with Mr Penney.

During the twelve months that followed, a million dollars' worth of editorial publicity was sparked off by this show, in newspapers and magazines all over the country. This was far in excess of anything Penney's had anticipated. And – to their amazement – the clothes sold, too.

I really believe that when the whole thing had first been planned, it had been looked upon purely as a promotional idea … to promote the idea in people's minds that Penney's were in fact an up-to-date, with-it kind of store. Actual sales had been regarded as irrelevant.

We had not fully understood this. We didn't really appreciate that, in the back of his mind, Paul Young was thinking of us as a one-shot thing. He changed his mind only when he saw the sales figures. For the first time in the history of Penney's, an Ambassador's wife shopped in one of their stores. Lady Ormsby-Gore bought one hundred and fifty dollars' worth of my clothes for her daughter. This was splendid.

Alexander and I stayed on in Washington for three or four days longer. Paul Young was with us. I had to make personal appearances at the Penney stores around Washington (where the weight of the initial publicity was concentrated); talk on the radio and appear on television. I began to get over my shyness; I had to.

Washington is an extraordinary place. Practically everyone seems to work for the State Department. Work starts at about seven-thirty in the morning and finishes about half-past four. Life is very formal. All kinds of protocol have to be observed.

The First Secretary gave a dinner party for us and I found out that the guest of honour at any formal party was expected to leave by 10 p.m. ... 10.30 at the very latest. We were puzzled by this because we wondered what on earth people did in the evenings. Both the restaurants shut down about half-past ten and there appeared to be nothing going on ... no life anywhere.

Then we discovered the coloured life. There are the most marvellous negro clubs that keep going all night with terrific swinging jazz. We had a secret ball!

We were given just one whole morning to ourselves to go out on our own and see the town. Penney's set a tight schedule on business trips, such a tight schedule that I have grown to expect five minutes specifically allocated for going to the loo.

We were in Georgetown when we flagged down a taxi and found it was being driven by the most enormous coloured woman.

Alexander said, 'Will you show us the town?'

'No,' she replied firmly. 'There are licensed guides to do that.'

She sat there, looking very solid, very tight-lipped, buttoned-up and unfriendly. It looked as if she would drive off without us at any minute. We got in quickly.

'In that case,' Alexander said, 'can we ask you to take us to the other side of town.'

Then we started chatting this woman up. She wasn't having any.

'I am not permitted to tell you anything,' she said. 'I am just a taxi driver.'

She began to thaw out a little only when Alexander mentioned President Kennedy's popularity in England.

'You're British, are you?' she said.

'Yes,' replied Alexander. 'And we have only this morning to look around.'

At that she opened out. Obviously she thought the world of the President and we became friends. It seemed as if she decided she liked us after all and to hell with the laws that said she must not act as a guide. We spent three hours with her driving round on the most highly coloured tour there can ever have been.

Next day we had to leave Washington for New York. We went on the shuttle service. It is a pretty casual arrangement. You arrive at the airport and if there happens to be a plane leaving with a vacant seat, you get on. You put your money in an old-fashioned ticket machine on board rather like the ones on old country buses and out comes a ticket.

There is none of the sleek airworthy look of the modern machine about these planes; they look as if they are on their last legs. Alexander is scared stiff of planes at any time. This was awful. We flew at what seemed to us to be about fifty feet from the ground barely skimming the tree tops; it was terribly bumpy and we lurched around blown about by the high winds.

Alexander was sitting beside an atomic scientist who spent the time working on a lot of strange and highly complicated hieroglyphics on the back of an old envelope. This man noticed how terrified Alexander was. He said to him, 'Don't worry. It's a bit bumpy because this is an old machine. This service has been running for years and they have never had a crash yet. I ought to know because I make this trip two or three times a week. Mind you, we turned over last week but they managed to get it right side up without too much trouble.'

I suppose he thought he was putting Alexander at ease! We were both a bit sweaty when we touched down at Idlewild.

We spent most of our time in New York going round meeting again all those people who had been so good to us on our first visit. We were beginning to have quite a few friends there. And we made a lot more.

With Steinberg's help we had started the Ginger Group and were doing a growing wholesale business in Britain. We had found out that we liked working with this firm and we hoped they liked working with us. It seemed logical to form a joint company with them so that we could sell clothes well designed but really cheap so that all the swinging chicks could have them. This had started well and Alexander was keen to introduce the Ginger Group to America.

We talked over our hopes and plans with Rosemary McMurtry

who came to have a drink with us and she said, 'O.K. If you're in mass production now, we will give you a tremendous spread.'

'That's wonderful of you,' Alexander replied. 'But how are we going to start? What sort of distribution would we have in the States? It is no good you giving us six colour pages in *Seventeen* if the clothes don't exist for the dollies to buy.'

Rosemary suggested that when we had the clothes ready, we should come again to New York. She would get in touch with all the stores who normally work with *Seventeen* on a promotion of this kind and would tell them that she planned to feature the clothes in the magazine.

When the time came for this promotion, Alexander returned to New York with the collection and found that Rosemary had invited buyers from seventy of the best fashion stores in America to *Seventeen* offices on Park Avenue for a special showing. She had hired half a dozen super model girls for the week Alexander was to be in New York, moved out of her own office so that he could use it and lent him three stenographers to write the orders for him. The show she organized was given in the large conference room which had been cleared for the purpose.

Alexander was knocked out by the kindness of the *Seventeen* girls and the trouble they took. They were marvellous to him. I think he was thoroughly spoilt!

The night he was leaving for London, he counted out his money and found that after paying his hotel bill, he had 170 dollars over. He put twenty dollars in his pocket to make sure he would get to the airport and went out and bought a crate of champagne for the girls to be delivered to Park Avenue with his love when he had taken off.

During the days he had been away I had been working like mad on the first collection we were to show in Paris the day after he got back to London.

The thought of Paris was even more frightening than New York. I had produced a group which we called 'The Wet Collection' using Poly-Vinyl-Chloride – it's what used to be called oilskin and, at that time, it had never been used for fashion. We planned to show this under the Bazaar banner and then to follow up with the Ginger Group collection which was being flown straight to Paris from America. The Ginger Group clothes were held up for two days by customs so they, in fact, were never shown. We had to concentrate on the Bazaar collection. We were lucky to have these. As usual they had been finished at the very last minute and, as always happened, we had forgotten to order the enormous trunks we should have had to transport the clothes to France. Once again, we had to make do with dozens of cardboard boxes and grocers' crates.

We must have looked like the Victorian idea of a world tour when we set off. We had five terrific model girls with us ... Penny Patrick, Mary Rose McNair, Jill Kennington, Vicki Vaughan and Jill Stinchcombe. It must have been quite a sight when we arrived at the airport; Alexander and George Kersen, our sales manager, and me surrounded by these gorgeous dollies swarming across the tarmac carrying on one elegant finger the tortoise-shell cases that contained their expensive false hair pieces. Behind came a string of porters carrying one cardboard crate after another. The people in the airport stopped to stand and stare at these beautiful girls prancing along with such an entourage.

We had taken the Crillon Hotel for the show. At least, that's what it felt like. All we really had was a huge suite there and lots of bedrooms and we had booked the enormous room on the ground floor for the show. This wasn't really the most suitable place as background for our clothes; it is tremendously ornate with masses of chandeliers and marble walls ... a staggering contrast to the extreme and outrageous clothes I had made.

Stimulated and probably over-excited by the success we were having in America and by the challenge of the Ginger Group, I had let myself go on this collection. Everything new I wanted to do, I did. I overdid it. It was the biggest 'Pay attention ... you can bloody well look at this' collection ever seen. I didn't *suggest* any-thing the way it is generally done in the more orthodox fashion trade. I went right ahead and did it. I have never enjoyed myself more making a collection. I think it hit everyone between the eyes; but we nearly came unstuck as a result of it. It was the least commercially successful collection I ever made.

Everyone of importance in the international fashion world was in Paris ... all the top fashion Press and the buyers ... because, the day before our show, the Fashion House Group of London had put on their first ever combined show in Paris which was a tremendously smart and glossy affair.

Ernestine Carter made sure that all the most important fashion editors of Paris and New York came to our show. We didn't know why at the time but we found out later.

We did our best to get everyone into a sympathetic frame of mind by serving lots of champagne the minute they arrived at the Crillon but we could not persuade any of them actually to drink it. They just went and sat firmly in the front rows waiting. They appeared to me that day to be the most frightening women in the world.

Then Lady Dixon, wife of the British Ambassador, arrived with her daughter. I knew that her attendance at the Fashion House Group show the day before had been considered a tremendous scoop and that the fact that she had turned up at our show would immediately arouse special interest. Anyway, she is the sister of one of Alexander's aunts which helped ...

Photographer John Cowan was with us again, this time to make a film of the show. He wanted to get the whole atmosphere of the thing and not just the clothes so he was shooting all over the place and going up to the grandees to take close-ups. I remember Ernestine Carter was frightfully embarrassed about being photographed and I think she was in two minds whether to make a scene or just tell John (whom she knows very well anyway) to stop it.

The nervous strain on us was colossal. Fortunately the model girls backed us up as they always do. They were marvellous. They were pretty nervous too but they didn't show it. They rose magnificently to the occasion.

The show went on at colossal speed with jazz playing in the background. We showed about sixty dresses and suits in fifteen minutes flat.

We just happened to have walked into Dee Wells in the Crillon that morning with her eleven-year-old daughter ... a very pretty leggy girl. I had asked Dee if she would allow her daughter to open the show for us. This she did, wearing a shiny mock-crocodile batwing top over black tights, her long fair hair hanging over her shoulders. She looked wild as she ran down the catwalk with the other girls, like greyhounds, pounding on behind. There were none of the mincing up and down, stop and start, stylized movements of the usual fashion model. These girls were all primarily photographic models so that when they stopped in their tracks, they automatically took up the sort of arrogant positions you see in the fashion pages of the glossies.

This type of showing was still something of a shock treatment. It had always been our way of showing but, at that time, none of the foreign fashion journalists had ever been to one of our shows.

I have always liked showing my clothes in this way and I am no longer alone in this. The description one journalist gave of the show at Courrèges this year might well have been a word picture of our first showing at Knightsbridge Bazaar. It was described as 'a display of far-out fashions that swung down the runways to the way-in beat of progressive jazz'.

When the clothes had all been seen there was, once again, the extraordinary stunned silence which seems to follow such a high speed show. There was not a sound in the room ... no one moved. Nothing could have been more frightening.

Then everyone got up and filed out, murmuring polite meaningless things and saying that they felt they must come and see it all again. They were so quiet and undemonstrative that we all thought the show had been a total failure. The most awful and sick-making feeling came over me. I had already found out that I wasn't very good at taking success; now I had to find out how I could face up to failure.

Alexander had to get back to London. I had to stay on at the Crillon alone to show again next day to the buyers. I went to bed. I was shaking all over. I felt sick. I could not sleep.

The next morning the telephone started ringing and it never stopped all day. It seemed that everyone who had been at the show the day before wanted to come in and see the clothes again. By now these were all hanging on rails in the suite we had at the Crillon and all day long I never let up for an instant.

Suddenly – and, to me, unaccountably – the whole picture was changed. Everyone was mad about the clothes. They said the most flattering things; they wanted to borrow garments for photography; they wanted to back us.

Listening to their comments and the wonderfully complimentary things they said, I knew the show was a success after all.

Elle and *Jardin des Modes* both decided to do four-page features on the clothes; there were endless write-ups in the British Press; *Life* magazine and *Seventeen* planned full-length features. The French fashion journalists were particularly enthusiastic. They knew all there is to know about the haute couture but they had never seen such extravagant and uncompromising clothes at such cheap prices.

I had hoped to catch an evening plane back to London to be in time for the first Ginger Group Press show at the May Fair Hotel the next day but with so much interest in the clothes and so many things happening and the phone ringing all the time, I missed every plane out of Paris that night.

The only thing to do was to catch the milk plane in the morning so that, with luck, I'd be at the May Fair by ten o'clock for the show. I could have rung up friends and gone out with them. With so many British and American photographers, model girls and fashion writers in Paris at the time, I could simply have walked along the Faubourg St-Honoré and met half a dozen people I knew and would normally have liked to spend an evening with.

Clare had made sure we knew everybody in the fashion world by this time and we had started the habit of visiting Paris regularly for the week-end immediately before the January and July collections started. We used to give a lunch party at our hotel, Le Relais Bisson, for between fourteen and twenty people on the Monday before the serious work was under way and everyone thought of this as rather a restful thing and a good start to the week.

There is an air of festivity in Paris at these times (it never seems to happen in London but that may perhaps be because we live here and it is never the same in one's own town) so it was always a fun week-end for us and we found it an easy way of meeting up with many of our overseas friends.

It cost us an enormously expensive lunch but it was terrific. Unfortunately we tend not to have time to do it now. Our guests would include people like Ernestine Carter, Eugenia Sheppard, Iris Ashley, Barbara Griggs, Sally Kirkland, Percy Savage, John Cowan, Jill Kennington, Norman Parkinson and so on.

Iris was the golden girl of the whole thing. She is the original epitome of the elegant fashion journalist. She really looked the part. Without looking round, we could always tell when Iris walked into the room. All the waiters would stop serving and look towards the door; they simply could not believe they would ever see an Englishwoman looking as Iris looked. She always made a tremendous entrance. The Frenchmen, sitting at other tables in the room, would stare at her; the women with them would stare at them.

Iris was the queen of the British fashion Press, an effect heightened by the fact that she always stayed at the Ritz and drove around in a chauffeur-driven car whilst most of the others had to take taxis, working like hell and staying at some cheap hotel in order to make out on their expense allowance.

Eugenia is a very striking person, too, but in an entirely different way from Iris. Barbara Griggs described her as 'probably the most feared journalist in Paris today whose pungent, outspoken column in the New York *Herald Tribune* has ruined a house's season before now because the American buyers read her and stayed away'.

She has this extraordinary energy; I don't think she ever goes to bed. I have never met anyone who knows how old she is but she could be sixteen in some respects in spite of the fact that she is the doyen of the American fashion Press. The first time we went to Small's Paradise, one of the Harlem night spots in New York, Eugenia was dancing away when we arrived. When we finally left, exhausted, she was still dancing.

Eugenia Sheppard has been marvellously good to us. Soon after Alexander and I got home from the launching of the Penney project in Washington, she called to see us in our scruffy little workroom in Chelsea. Afterwards she did a tremendous piece about us in the New York *Herald Tribune*. She gave this the headline 'Before and After Quant' which was rather fun. She said there was a revolution going on and people were on one side or the other; they were what she described as Before or After. And she said I was really very like Coco Chanel in lots of ways which, coming from Eugenia Sheppard, was an exciting thing for me to read. She is a great friend of Sally Kirkland, *Life* magazine's famous fashion editor.

Sally isn't the easiest guest at a lunch party; she just isn't all that interested in food. We always think Le Relais Bisson has the most marvellous food. We used to brag about it a lot so, to justify our bragging, we always made a special effort to order all the most marvellous dishes for which the place is famous when we gave a party.

I remember at one of these how Sally listened to the grand head waiter reeling off all the delicious things on the menu with horror on her face.

Suddenly she said, 'Just give me a club sandwich, will you?'

I said, 'Oh, Sally, you simply must try some of this gorgeous food. Have a lobster soufflé or something.'

But Sally repeated, 'Just give me a club sandwich.'

The head waiter, very French, was horrified. He tried desperately to explain politely that they did not have that sort of thing. Eventually he had to admit that he didn't even know what a club sandwich was.

'Well, just bring me some cold meat, for heaven's sake,' Sally insisted in that American, gravelly voice of hers.

The poor man disappeared looking as if nothing more awful than this could ever happen to him. When he came back, he had some pâté de foie gras on a plate. It was the only 'cold' meat they had. He did his best to put it down in front of her politely.

Sally took a bite.

'For Christ's sake!' she screamed. 'All I ask for is cold meat.

And you bring me *bad* meat!'

She flung aside this absolutely delicious pâté and plunged into Ernestine's lobster soufflé.

I could have done with some of Sally's company that evening in the Crillon. But I hadn't the strength even to pick up the telephone. It was late and I was too whacked to do anything. I was alone in this great enormous suite suffering from a severe case of exhaustion. But I knew if I didn't force myself to do something about it, I would probably collapse altogether. I realized it would be sense to try and get something to eat.

I went down to the Grillroom. The place was practically deserted. I sat alone in one corner, still feeling desperately sick and trying to force myself to swallow. I couldn't get over the happenings of the day. Everyone had been so wildly friendly and flattering. I ordered a hamburger which seemed to be the easiest thing as I felt sure the waiters were longing to go off duty.

There was one other person in the room ... obviously an American ... and in the friendly, impersonal way of Americans, he came over to my table and asked if I would allow him to bring his coffee over and sit with me. So far as I was concerned, this was heaven-sent. I desperately needed something to take my mind off all that had happened during the day. And it turned out that he was feeling in much the same state of mind. He had had high-powered meetings all day, ending up with some enormous party at the American Embassy and he, too, was suffering from this great climactic thing which comes of being boosted up and then deflated by the aftermath. We were both thoroughly tee-ed up and at the same time flat.

He proved to be the most wonderful of companions: Senator William Benton, Ambassador to E.F.T.A., President of Joyce Shoes, *Encyclopaedia Britannica*, Benton and Bowles (the advertising agency) fame ... a tremendous personality.

We talked and talked until it became quite obvious that we really were being a nuisance to the waiters. Then we went up to his suite ... practically the whole of the first floor front of the Crillon. It looked more like the rooms in a palace than a hotel suite. Senator

Benton told me that when President Woodrow Wilson stayed at the Crillon, it was the suite he occupied with his staff.

Bill Benton was also catching an early morning plane; we both had to leave the hotel about five in the morning and as it was then long after midnight, it seemed pointless going to bed. I would not have been able to sleep anyway and I was utterly absorbed in all I was hearing.

Bill Benton has a tremendous history. As a young man of twenty he married and, when he graduated, he stayed on at his university to teach. Whilst he was teaching, some firm approached the university to try and persuade them to buy the *Encyclopaedia Britannica*. Very little money was being asked for it but, in spite of this, the project was turned down.

Bill Benton was only a junior professor and earning very little money but somehow he managed to get the backing he needed and he bought the *Encyclopaedia*. That was his start. From there he went on to build up the tremendous worldwide business interests he now controls.

His way of working and keeping in touch with every part of his empire was a revelation to me. Everything is done by word of mouth. In every room of his suite I saw the most advanced electronic equipment installed to record every word he spoke. Wherever he goes he takes a team of secretaries. Their first job every morning is to remove the tapes from the machines, type out the recordings and dispatch the relevant letters and reports to the different directors and managers. We recorded all our conversation that night ... the poor secretaries!

I still get letters from him and more often than not they will have been 'dictated in Moscow and transcribed in New York'. Over the years we have kept up that extraordinary conversation and exchange of ideas started by chance in the Crillon Grillroom.

He sent me a full set of *Encyclopaedia Britannica* and sometimes when he is more than usually busy I receive just the shortest note saying some such thing as 'refer to pages so and so'. In this way we carry on the most dotty international correspondence and have rows and arguments and discussions through the pages of the *Encyclopaedia*.

He provided just the right sensational ending to what had proved to be three most sensational days for me. It should have set the seal of success on the whole thing. But this was not to be. In spite of all the superb support we had from the Press, we soon realized what we were up against.

In Poly-Vinyl-Chloride we had used a revolutionary new material before anyone had had time to find out and solve the difficulties of mass production. We were not the first to find out that it doesn't always pay to be first in the field. The pioneer is the one who makes the mistakes, discovers the snags and prepares the ground for those who more cautiously follow after.

P.V.C. had never been tested for mass production manufacture. We began to come up against the most ghastly difficulties. All the engineering work that ought to have been done before the clothes were shown ... the experiments on welding seams ... had been overlooked. When the stuff was put on an ordinary machine, the vinyl stuck to the foot or melted, and when we found a way of stopping this, the seams were perforated like those of a postage stamp and ripped at the slightest provocation. It was obvious that welding was the only possible process of manufacture and there was no suitable machinery for this. We ought to have been in touch with one of the big firms experienced in making macintoshes but we were still too amateur in our approach to have looked this far ahead.

We had had so much publicity that the clothes were in enormous demand and we simply could not deliver. We fell down all along the line on production. It was disastrous. Everyone wanted our things and we did not know how to make them.

Alexander and I spent all our time on planes rushing between London, New York and Paris, sampling, making experiments, but with no success. It took us nearly two years to perfect the process whereby the seams of P.V.C. can be held fast in a satisfactory way and by that time other designers on both sides of the Channel were as bewitched as I still am with this super shiny man-made stuff and its shrieking colours, its vivid cobalt, scarlet and yellow, its gleaming liquorice black, white and ginger.

This was the worst season we have had to live through. We made losses for the first time in our lives simply because we could not keep up with the thing we had started. But one wonderful thing happened. One afternoon when I was in conference with some film directors and producers discussing the clothes I was to make for an American film, the telephone rang in the office. Alexander answered it. It was Ernestine Carter. When Alexander explained what I was doing, she said, 'Oh, it doesn't matter. I just wanted her to know that she has won the *Sunday Times* Fashion Award!'

When Alexander told me, I pretty nearly fainted. We had never thought of this even as a remote possibility. We thought the Award must inevitably go to a couturier. I rang Ernestine at once. All I could do was to thank her. I was too overwhelmed to talk sense. It was the greatest thing she could possibly have done for us. I knew it was she who had said to the other judges ... Helene Gordon Lazareff, Eleanor Lambert, Diana Vreeland and Marie Louise Bousquet ... 'You must come and see Mary Quant because she is the one I would like to nominate for the British Award.' I knew that it had to be a unanimous decision of all the international judges and I understood now why Ernestine had brought so many distinguished fashion journalists to my show in Paris.

The presentation of the Awards by Lord Thomson and the Countess of Dalkeith took place at the London Hilton. It was one of the most nerve-racking days of my life. Ernestine had organized the most tremendous show and about three thousand people turned up for it ... all the top people of the fashion industry of the world, including all our competitors. The thing was heavily over-subscribed and we only just managed to get two tickets for my parents.

Amongst other things, I was showing the 'Wet Collection' which had been shown in Paris for the first time a few weeks previously. We rehearsed for two days beforehand and all the time rehearsals were going on we were being interviewed and photographed, filmed and televised. It was a shattering experience.

A huge team of models had been hired by the *Sunday Times*. And, under the direction of Michael Whittaker, the most enormously elaborate show was licked into shape. I would really have liked to use my favourite girls who know my stuff well and have done so many shows for us in our jazzy and casual way but the whole thing had to be worked out like a military operation and it just was not possible.

The nerve-racking thing for me was that although Pierre Cardin and Norman Novell were showing expensive couture clothes, none of my things cost more than twelve guineas and most of them were around the five pound mark! I had to keep reminding myself that this was the whole point of what we were doing. At all events, Novell was just as nervous as me and he tremblingly held my hand while his collection was shown.

Ernestine was in very much the same state. We had been asked to lunch at the French Embassy immediately before the presentation and we went together. On the way she lost the notes of the speech she was to make that afternoon, which didn't help.

We found practically all the other guests at this lunch were French. I had never before met any really grand Frenchwomen and I found them quite terrifying. They were extremely formal, tremendously dressed up, rigidly correct. Ernestine and I had been working like mad all morning; I was still wearing the scruffy old working shirt and skirt I had put on for rehearsals; and I had no hat. In the surroundings of the Embassy, I was completely overwhelmed. But I cheered up a bit when one of the Embassy footmen pinched my bottom!

I was introduced, in French, to various people who all appeared to be sitting on the very edge of their chairs with dead straight backs, sipping at the drinks they held in an incredibly ladylike way. A vacant chair was found for me and as I was being introduced to my immediate neighbour, I thought the name I heard was Schiaparelli. I couldn't believe I had heard correctly although she looked exactly as I had always imagined the great Schiaparelli' – wearing dusty black and a 1930 turban, and with ankles that seemed to go straight into the stocky-heeled shoes they wore in those days. She was the complete reincarnation of my idea of fashion in the thirties.

I have always been a tremendous fan of Schiaparelli but I had thought of her as dead. Whether some indication of the thought in my mind showed in my face or whether it was because, in my terror, I made some particularly fatuous remark, I was promptly squashed. I sat there miserably, not daring to speak again and absolutely certain that, so far as Schiaparelli was concerned, I was a dead loss. She had no possible way of knowing how thrilled I was to meet her.

When we went into luncheon, I looked at the seating plan and there was my name, once again next to Madame Schiaparelli. I felt terrible about it. This woman had obviously taken against me; she had already absolutely flattened me. There was about ten minutes of the most awful silence between us. Then I thought, 'This is no good. I'm a failure with her anyway. I might just as well jabber away.'

I decided I would tell her about my visit to Debenham's fur storage vaults a couple of days earlier. Austin Garrett, with whom I was working on the first collection of fur coats I designed for Debenham's, had taken me to see these. I think they must stretch under the ground half-way down Wigmore Street. They are huge. It is the strangest place. The temperature is that of a butcher's deep freeze and you have to put on a greatcoat rather like Arctic clothing before you go in.

The place is full of fur coats, most of which have been there for years. Some of them have been there for over forty years since the days when Russian grandees, escaping to Britain from the Revolution, deposited them for safety, leaving behind banker's orders to pay the storage charges more or less in perpetuity. Quite a number of the tremendously rich International Set seem to store their coats and then forget about them. I saw the most staggering men's coats made to go right down to the ground and obviously worn at one time by some terrific Tartar types who must have been at least seven foot tall. Some of them were made of a heavy, shaggy type of suède, appliquéd with inset pieces of coloured suèdes embroidered in position, and completely lined with great heavy furs which looked to me like racoon.

I was fascinated by everything I saw. But nothing excited or fascinated me more than the Schiaparelli coats. I suppose they must have been made in the nineteen-twenties and thirties. Some of them have sleeves with enormous puffs to the elbow and then tapered down tightly to the wrist. These coats are cut full length to the ankles and are beautifully fitted and waisted. Her velvet cloaks, completely lined with fur, absolutely took my breath away. I was simply riveted by them. Austin Garrett had to drag me away. Left on my own, I think I would have stayed until I was frozen solid in the deep freeze.

I started telling Madame Schiaparelli all this and how excited I had been at seeing her coats. This broke the ice. We made friends and for the rest of the lunch we were shouting and jabbering away together and having a hilarious time. We really hit it off and by the time we got to the last course we were practically dominating the lunch party because, having started, she went on to tell all sorts of marvellous stories about the thirties. She told me so many of the things I had always wanted to know about fashion in those days. She is the most fascinating woman and, because of her, it turned out to be the most wonderful lunch party for me in spite of my bad start.

A matter of weeks after this, I was told I had been elected a 'woman of the year'. This was another honour I had never expected. I was absolutely thrilled but terrified, too, because I was told I would have to make a speech. I had never made a speech of any kind before and this one was to be in front of an audience of women which made it even worse.

As the day drew near, I found I couldn't sleep, I couldn't eat, I couldn't do anything. I was in a terrible state. I was expected to speak on 'Is Happiness a Lost Art?' The more I thought about it, the more quickly every rational thought went from my head.

We decided it was obviously going to be impossible for me to make any attempt at a serious speech, so, together, Alexander and I settled on a ridiculous theme which we hoped would send the whole thing up. We brewed up a cynical list of all the things which people think one needs for happiness today. We decided a straightforward list would be the most foolproof thing for me to read.

Alexander drove me to the Savoy for the lunch. I was in a terrible state of nerves. And I wasn't helped by the fact that the man on the door wouldn't let me in. I had left my invitation at home. I hadn't forgotten it. I just thought I wouldn't need it. And I wasn't wearing a hat. I found it impossible to convince anyone that a 'woman of the year' would turn up at a lunch like that without a hat. I don't suppose I looked very convincing. I was wearing one of our five guinea dresses. I was finally rescued by someone who recognized me, thank goodness, and I discovered I was sitting between Mrs Harold Wilson and Beryl Grey.

It was an enormous banquet ... course after course. And I couldn't eat a thing. I simply could not swallow. I sat there rearranging the food on my plate so that it would look as if I had eaten some of it. All I could do was to drink the wine and I went on sipping this practically continuously. I was soon a bit cut because I hadn't eaten anything for days.

The awful moment came; I heard my name and I had to stand on my feet. I read our list:

I don't believe that happiness is a lost art; I don't believe it is an art at all.

It is simply that the accepted symbols of happiness have changed.

In the nineteenth century, a woman accepted her lot as a happy one if ...

> she had a husband who didn't beat her every day;
> her children were a credit to her;
> she was allowed to join in the conversation at dinner ...
> at least until the port arrived and the talk became
> interesting.

Now' – it would seem – for a woman to be happy she must have ...

a career ... a spindryer ... diamonds ... T.V. ...
a mink-lined macintosh ... a lover ... an electric toaster...
good health ... pep-up pills and sedatives ...
two cars (at least!) ... Jane Fonda's face and Simone de
Beauvoir's intellect ... a working knowledge of child
psychology ... a child ... a husband who beats her every
Friday.

The modern woman's standards seem to be mostly material ... but
then they always were.

The happy woman of the past took pleasure in:

the size of her house;
the status of her husband;
her own ability to make marmalade or something.

If that woman was happy she must have been a vegetable. What
is more ... I put it to you that she was not only not happy but she
wasn't even enjoying herself very much. She only thought she was
happy because this is what she had been brought up to hope for.

I believe that happiness (like misery) is an extreme emotion
that cannot be achieved by steering a middle course. It is an inci-
dental that takes us by surprise and the more we pursue it, the
less likely we are to achieve a moment of absolute happiness. Such
moments always take us by surprise ... often we don't recognize
them until they are over.

In fact, the exciting treat we have looked forward to ... or
the achievement of an ambition ... leaves one with a feeling of
anticlimax.

For me – anyway – the happiest moments of life have been,
for instance:

eating baked beans in the middle of the night;
teaching two policemen the Bossa Nova;
and finishing this awful speech.

All this wasn't meant very seriously and it wasn't taken seriously. I felt that at a lunch like that, the last thing anyone would want from someone like me was a pompous deep analysis.

It is strange that these two outstanding milestones in my life ... the *Sunday Times* Fashion Award and being elected a 'woman of the year' – should both have turned up in the season which was to prove our biggest commercial flop. It was all too much: too much excitement on one side; too much worry on the other. Archie and Alexander felt the strain as much as I did. We were all absolutely played out.

The business had grown too quickly for us; it had become such a very complicated thing. First we had one shop in the King's Road; then we had a second one in Brompton Road. We had two wholesale companies going full time. I had had to learn to live with four deadlines constantly looming just ahead of me (four for Bazaar, four for the Ginger Group) quite apart from all the growing overseas commitments.

There was always pressure ... always people waiting to see us ... wanting to talk to us. Instead of being two small-time people venturing into the fringe of the fashion world by selling clothes in Chelsea and Knightsbridge, we were selling in real quantities in America and everywhere else.

It was the sheer size of the business that was so frightening. In the old days, if I produced a dud dress, we would be left with about thirty of these on our hands. We would just mark them right down and get rid of them in the sale.

If I produce a dud dress now and this goes into production (which has to be done before even a store buyer has seen it ... let alone the woman who is going to buy it) this can mean a couple of thousand lousy dresses on our hands. One is surrounded by vast quantities of risk money all the time.

There is this enormous weight of responsibility. All the time I am designing, I am asking myself, 'Am I right? Am I right to persuade everyone to use these super swinging model girls I love? Is this something that will creep into the clothes ... this idealized idea of what a woman's shape should be?'

We are working with great mass production commercial firms. They want new ideas all the time but in a curious way I find there is a built-in resistance to anything really new. At first they could not, and would not, understand that new ideas demand new fabrics and new fabrics demand new methods of manufacture, new ways of presentation, new ways of approaching buyers.

It seemed to me in these early days that manufacturers thought it was sufficient to stick the name of a new young designer on a garment and then serve it up as before. It is never as easy as that. It is essential that the manufacturer should contribute a great deal of new thinking too.

All this meant that quite apart from the strain of designing in continuous succession, we were having to cajole and persuade and battle for every one of the things we wanted and knew we had to produce if we were to keep the reputation we had been lucky enough to get. It was one long battle all the time.

In 'big' business so many people are absolutely terrified of doing anything original; it is too much of a challenge. They are content to sit back on the reputation they have already acquired. They seem to be terrified of having to use their brains and start something completely new; to apply the methods and invest the money they've got in anything untried and without precedent. They want new ideas but without risk and without having to sacrifice the old. It is far easier for young people like us because we are starting from scratch anyway. We are not set in our ways. We have no past successes to fall back on.

Trying to find a working compromise between the old idea of solidarity and our idea of trying anything new was a terrific strain. We seemed to be running all the time just to keep up with ourselves. Strain mounted up upon strain. It was a vicious circle. The more we worried, the more exhausted we got. And the more exhausted we were, the more we worried. If one has too much to do, one tends to do all of it badly rather than some of it well.

Fashion is a frightening business to be in; all the time you have to force yourself to think ahead; you have to try to think further ahead than anyone else. If you can't do this, you know you are going to cease to count. You are endlessly trying to produce something absolutely new ... and on a deadline.

Then the bigger an organization grows, the more a business develops, the greater become all the problems of management. These increase with every success and, on top of them, come the ever-increasing difficulties of finding the right people to work with you and co-operate successfully with others advanced enough in their own thinking to contribute original ideas for development.

Every one of these things is vitally important. If you fall down on any one of them, the whole thing is liable to collapse.

I am practically never ill, physically, but I knew at this time that I was nearer to breaking point than even Alexander suspected. The only sort of relief we ever got from high pressure work was when we reverted to the slightly dotty amusements of our young days together. To some extent this was a safety valve to us even then.

We had a flat at the top of a building in Eaton Place at the time. It was the Fifth of November. Alexander had bought a whole pile of the most expensive rockets and fireworks, rather hoping we would be asked to some party or other. As it happened, no one invited us to a Guy Fawkes party that year. We just sat in the apartment feeling rather neglected and let-down. We decided we would have our own party. We put a big bucket of water on the small balcony outside one window and Alexander lobbed the rockets off one by one high over Eaton Square and the King's Road. He really put on a terrific show. It was rather sad that I was the only one there to see it.

Gradually the flat got more and more full of the backwash of smoke. It became impossible to see across the room. The whole place was full of that marvellous Fifth of November smell. Then the police arrived. As Alexander answered the door, the smoke billowed out on to the landing.

'We have had a complaint that someone in the neighbourhood is letting off fireworks,' one of them said. 'You wouldn't be doing that, would you, sir?'

'Oh, no,' said Alexander, waving his arms frantically across his face to clear a little of the smoke so that he could see who he was talking to.

'We felt sure it would not be you,' these enchanting policemen said. 'We are sorry to have disturbed you.'

Another time when the police came to the apartment, they were not so understanding … quite rightly! Alexander and I had had a ghastly row. I haven't the slightest idea what started it now but I know Alexander stumped out of the flat and disappeared. He told me the next day that he had gone to Brown's Hotel and stayed the night there but of course I could not know this at the time. When he awoke in the morning, he found he had only a pound note in his notecase and very little loose change so at about nine o'clock he came back to the flat. He found he couldn't get in because I had double-locked the door.

He thought I must still be sleeping so he went to the Tate Gallery, wandered round looking at the pictures, then came back to the flat. It was about eleven o'clock by this time and I should have left for the office ages ago to keep various appointments I had for that day.

Alexander tried the door again. The lock still would not move. He banged the door. No answer. He went downstairs and telephoned. No reply.

Suddenly he realized just what a nasty row it had been. We really had said some foul things to each other. The thought struck him that perhaps I had taken too many sleeping pills. He was absolutely terrified, so terrified that he says he just stood still and did nothing for several minutes. Then it came to him that if anything had gone wrong, something had better be done about it – and quickly. He rushed to the police station and said to the man on duty, 'Listen, please. I can't get into my flat and I am rather worried about my wife's condition.'

'Yes, sir,' the officer on duty said politely but without moving. 'Perhaps you will take a seat?'

No one appeared to register the fact that this was an emergency call. Alexander was in a panic by this time. At last another policeman came into the room and said in a leisurely way, 'The thing to do, sir, is to call the fire brigade.'

Alexander begged him to get on with it at once. Call the fire brigade and any other brigade that might help. The whole thing was explained in great detail over the phone. Everything moved dead slow. Alexander convinced himself I was either dead or dying.

Eventually about seven fire engines arrived in Eaton Square with all the impressive turntable machinery. But Alexander was so frantic by this time that he convinced them the quickest way to get into the place was to batter down our front door. This they did.

Alexander's panic had become infectious. The firemen caught the feeling. Once inside the flat, Alexander hoped they would go. He wanted to face this thing on his own. But not a bit of it. The firemen were determined that having got this far they were going to see the thing through if only so that they could write a full report for their records. Alexander had a job to persuade them to let him go into our bedroom alone.

It was a terrible anticlimax when he saw me sitting up in bed perfectly normal except that I was still absolutely furious. He had the awful job of explaining to the infuriated firemen who by this time had been joined by several policemen.

The one in charge said, 'I am afraid we shall have to insist on seeing Mrs Plunket Greene, sir. Got to make sure the wife's all right.'

Alexander said, 'Well, if you must, you must. But I don't advise it. You may hear language such as you have never heard before. Believe me, everything is all right. I am most grateful to you. Have a drink? Have anything you like. But please go away!'

After they had gone, we both burst out laughing. It was disgraceful of us to have behaved in this way. But it was all so utterly ridiculous. We went out to lunch together to celebrate.

All the same we began to notice that, in our desperation to keep our heads in important matters, we distracted ourselves by flying off the handle about any trivial matter that could be used as an excuse to release our pent-up feelings.

We both became incapable of accepting even constructive

criticism from our colleagues and worked off the anxiety bred by our exhaustion by picking quarrels over idiotic differences of opinion. We made ourselves thick smokescreens to hide the fact that we were overwhelmed.

To me, every small detail of my work seemed climactic. Every detail of my job seemed to be the one that would make us or break us. I so lost my sense of proportion that I would worry and fret about things like an unmanufacturable sleeve in a suit that I had designed in an unavailable cloth which was, anyway, too late for the buyers to buy.

Alexander rushed about giving lavish parties to promote new designs which we had failed to get made and whenever these things were photographed in the newspapers, the stores, who had eagerly awaited promised deliveries, lost heart and cancelled their orders.

Actually it was not all as hopeless as this although Archie was forced to point out, rather sourly, that we always seemed to spend a hundred and fifty pounds to make a hundred. Things went from bad to worse. Occasionally one of my maddest designs would sell like mad, things would get a little better and we would celebrate wildly.

It was in a short calm period between euphoria and despair, when we had our vision temporarily in focus, that Alexander and I decided we had each better get the help of a psychiatrist. I suppose we both made a lucky choice and I have to resist rushing about recommending analysis to all and sundry in the way newly married couples recommend marriage to bachelors.

All the same it is worth saying that the self-discovery ... the finding out what makes one tick ... the learning to make the best of whatever one's abilities may be ... the whole thing ... is an education. It is like learning to swim only a thousand times more valuable (unless you happen to be shipwrecked!).

I now find myself able to cope with pretty well anything and able, too, to do ten times as much as I could and do each thing ten times more capably.

Nothing worries me any more because I know that worry is an abortive process. I can cogitate and plan, concentrate on difficult problems and recognize the impossible without panic. I can sit calmly in a taxi on the way to delivering a speech to the bigwigs of our industry knowing that even if I talk a load of irrelevant rubbish, I will do the best I can and that is the best I can hope for.

I suppose it sounds smug but, in fact, I am like the girl in the commercial who says, 'Don't thank me ... thank Horlick's ... Lifebuoy ... Ex-Lax' or whatever it is.

So long as I can remember my ambition has been to be a designer. This, in itself, is not enough. There must be thousands of talented designers in this country who have never got going because they have never had the chance to cultivate this thing that enables any one person to enthuse others. No one can achieve anything on their own. A designer who is to succeed must have a team of people who believe in her so much that they are prepared to make a tremendous personal effort to carry out her ideas. A designer has got to be able to talk convincingly to people as well as put down her ideas on paper. She has got to be able to persuade others to go along with her even at times against their own inclinations. And ... as often as possible ... she has got to be right.

I know now that however emotionally involved I am in anything I am doing, I dare not allow myself one ounce of prima donna behaviour. As soon as you give way to this, you have the mistrust of the business people, the manufacturers, the buyers, the retailers, the promoters. Any one of these people who may see prima donna behaviour going on is at once uneasy. And there was a time when I allowed it to be obvious to everyone that I was amateur and unprofessional in my approach to administration and organization.

I haven't mastered complete self-control yet. Sometimes when we get home, Alexander still has to reassure me, over and over again, that I have said and done the right thing.

Sometimes when I do a drawing for a newspaper at a moment's notice, people will remark on how quickly and easily it is done. What they don't know is that it can be done quickly only because of the days and nights of thinking that have preceded it. A design lies in my mind for days, perhaps for weeks, then, when the demand comes, it matures, on the moment, out of hours of thought. It is not, in fact, anything like as spontaneous as it appears.

I have had to learn not to waste thinking time. It is not necessary to be writing or drawing all the time but you must always be thinking. If you have really thought anything out to the last detail, it can be put on paper in a matter of minutes. Any sudden demand acts like a shot of adrenalin and makes it just that much more exciting.

I give the impression that my best work is done only when I am under pressure. What is not understood is that what I produce at the last minute is the climax of all I have done before. The best work is done at the end because of all you have learned from earlier mistakes. Sudden, urgent demand brings into sharp focus all the things you have been thinking about often quite unconsciously. Everything falls into place.

But, quite apart from designing clothes, I have to do a lot of other things, too. They are all more or less important and one needs to keep one's head.

A fairly typical day in my life might go like this:

10.00 a.m.	Take last night's sketches to the workroom and discuss them with the cutters.
11.00 a.m.– 12.30 p.m.	See the ranges from six or seven cloth merchants for a collection which will go into the shops nine months later.
12.30 p.m.	Tom Wolsey to discuss the designs of labels and swing tickets for a new range for America.
1.00 p.m.	Choose trimmings from a selection made by our cloth buyer.
1.15 p.m.	Lunch in the restaurant round the corner with Archie, Alexander and the managing director of a hosiery firm who want to produce Quant stockings.
2.30 p.m.	To Youthlines to look at the first samples of the new underwear made to my drawings.

3.15 p.m.	To the Ginger Group to meet Canadian journalists doing a piece about us.
4.00 p.m.	Vidal Sassoon.
5.15 p.m.	Back to workroom to see latest dresses tried on by Jan de Souza or Sarah Dawson.
5.30 p.m.	Austin Garrett brings some skins for the next furs.
6.30 p.m.	Home. Drinks with the design director of the Butterick pattern company who publish my things from time to time.
8.00 p.m.	Dinner chez Rendlesham.
10.00 p.m.	The Purley Ball.

And – apart from this – I may have to talk to dozens of people on the telephone from journalists and licensees to cloth mills and scientists developing new materials for us.

The thing about a day like this is that, quite apart from the maddening frustrations of trying to move from one part of London to another in a limited time, I am not stationary – physically or mentally – for any length of time in any one place.

My mind has to switch from the clothes I am itching to design at this moment to those I will be doing six, even twelve, months ahead.

In a Press interview, I have to try to turn my thoughts back six months or more to the way I was thinking when I made the dresses designed then and currently being shown to the fashion journalists and buyers before going into the shops. I have to try to cut my mind off completely from all the ideas seething there for collections which will not be seen for another six months because it is obviously important that I do not disclose too soon the new colours, new shapes, new line, beginning to come to life on the drawing board.

The awful thing is having to follow through on things in the past far behind the way I am thinking at the moment and get back into an almost forgotten mood and an old way of thinking. I have to force myself to remember what I said last time and try to be consecutive.

If all the decisions I have to make in one day affected just one period of time, I don't think it would bother me too much. It is not that I have too many engagements; it is this going back and forward in time and switching my thoughts on and off. It is the terrifying concentration I have to give to so many different things which simply must not be forgotten.

Going from one place to another in a taxi now I find I am able to make my mind an absolute blank for a few minutes, then concentrate on what lies ahead without worrying about what has gone before. I can take each separate thing on its own and concentrate on this to the exclusion of all else so that when a problem is in front of me, I can fix my mind on this and get one thing settled at a time. It saves all the exhaustion I used to feel when I was trying to solve numberless queries all at the same time – a practice which, for me, inevitably results in utter confusion.

I understand that I can't have all I want the moment I want it. I have a little more understanding of the frustrations of big business particularly in the fashion world. If a terrific idea comes to me that calls for a fabric that does not exist, the thing is so rationalized in my mind that I am able to understand (and accept without too much fuss) that I must drop it. I must forget it for the time being ... hold it back in my mind and see if the idea is still relevant in a year's time when we have got everything else geared to keep up with it.

It still hurts – holding back on an idea – but I am able to accept the inevitable without fussing. I know that I simply cannot achieve my purpose without help and guidance and without the technical and professional advice and skill of the manufacturers and it has got to be a fifty-fifty deal. I have to give way when they are up against it and they have to meet me when it is at all possible.

It used to make me mad when garments I designed with slim-fitting sleeves came off the production lines with sleeves so tight they were impossible to wear with comfort. I did not understand that a sleeve that is well fitting on a model girl will probably look – and feel – tight on others.

Presumably a master like Balenciaga ... the absolute genius of cutting ... has no difficulty in producing a sleeve that anyone can put her arm into and lift comfortably above her head whilst it remains narrow-looking and slim in effect. But this is a difficult thing to do; it is an art, almost impossibly complicated when you are thinking in mass production terms.

Tricks of the trade in designing can make all the difference between success and failure. Chanel is a marvellous exponent of these on the grand scale. What I admire most about the Chanel look is that appearance comes first, then the clothes. The essence of Chanel is ease ... she always manages to achieve a casual, understated, almost haphazardly 'thrown together' effect which completely disguises the fact that all her clothes are the result of meticulous study, distinctive detail and a strategic tailoring that gives flowing, flawless fit.

Colour plays a tremendously important part. Since the very early King's Road Bazaar days I have been aware of the illusion you can get with this ... it is every bit as strong as the illusion of 'line'. Some colours always look more expensive than others. We can show a dress in pink or blue and it may look like nine guineas but if we show the same dress in tobacco brown or a soft beige or a deep purple, it immediately becomes a much more expensive-looking garment. Over and over again I've seen colour having an influence on even the most experienced of buyers.

When I first asked the manufacturers to give me crêpe in young colours, they said it was impossible and when I saw the samples they first produced, I felt they were right. Then I discovered that for some reason crêpe always starts out in a gloomy shade of grey. Dyed in this natural state, the grey always seeps through. Once I managed to persuade the manufacturers to bleach before dyeing, we got the absolutely clear, zooming colours I wanted.

In spite of this, the first collection I produced in crêpe was not a mad success but we did start a steady demand and this has grown bigger and bigger so that British manufacturers simply can't produce enough of it now and some has to be bought from America.

Then flannel caught my eye. I had been asked to design a dress in the Welsh stuff for a Swansea show during Eisteddfod week and I was shown some Welsh fabrics by Emrys Davis. Up till then, I had thought of flannel in terms of various shades of grey. I hadn't really considered other colours such as you see in club and school blazers as fashion possibles. It was only when I saw the clear colours it is possible for the mills to produce that flannel became the theme of a winter collection. Lots of customers, bored with grey flannel dresses and suits, fell madly in love with it.

It is this sort of thing that gives fashion its excitement. Over and over again it happens. Suddenly there's a new sensation. If it is not in colour, it may well be in fabric ... a new texture with a new lightness and a new 'feel' ... a fabric that looks exciting, feels exciting and makes for exciting fashion.

The breaking of traditional rules is always exciting. Rules are made to be broken. When you break a rule, you automatically arrive at something different and this is fun. Take stripes, checks and polka dots. For years these were worn on their own or teamed with a plain colour. Nobody asked why. I believe in mixing patterns and colours wildly. So far as I am concerned, spots go with stripes and checks.

One season I fell for feathers ... maybe a reflection of the present trend for plumage rivalry between the sexes (flying feathers have always been a feature of the mating ritual of birds). But feathers are fattening on the human ... as fattening as a diet of plum pudding.

But fur is not a prestige status symbol so far as I am concerned. It should be for everybody; the college set as well as the rich and the raffiné. A fur coat should be treated just like any other coat in everyday life. The tough, short-haired kind – musquash, pony, Dunkaly kid, nutria, racoon, persian and beaver lamb – all stand up to this kind of treatment. A fur coat should be casual, dateless ... my own favourite is the belted, trench-coat sort of thing. Whether this is made of mink or nutria or just P.V.C. it is plain sexy. Movie moguls discovered it; Garbo,

Dietrich and Bardot have all demonstrated it; and people who like my clothes, like it.

Rightly or wrongly, I have been credited with the Lolita Look, the Schoolgirl Look, the Wet Weather Look, the Kinky Look, the Good Girl Look and lots of others and it is said that I was first with knickerbockers, gilt chains, shoulderstrap bags and high boots. I like being given the credit for such things. I want to be first with a lot more. I want to invent new ways of making clothes in new materials, with new shapes and new fashion accessories that are up to date with the changing ways of life.

I never know when – or where – inspiration will come. This is one of the reasons why we have to be on the go each moment of the time.

The Garbo revival inspired in me the feminine, frilly look. I saw every single film of hers shown in the revival season. I thought she looked absolutely marvellous, quite shattering. In a flash I was tired of the arrogant 'beat' look, the look that seemed to say, 'I'm dressed like a boy and I'm as good as a boy'. I wanted my clothes to say, 'Girls are nothing like boys. I'm a girl and isn't it super?' Garbo made me want to concentrate on clothes that move rather than those that stand still.

When I saw Rudolf Nureyev – dashing, sweatered, very Russian-looking – he made me want to toss out every one of the lean, mean things I had in my collections. Suddenly I was sick of them all. I wanted a great, husky, generous shape … a big top with a short, straight skirt … a kind of off-stage Nureyev look.

I found inspiration in Goldfinger, too. Shirley Eaton sparked off the idea. Seeing her, I realized how terribly sexy the all-over pale gold look is … just the thing for girls out for a quick killing. If you saw Marlene Dietrich in her lone season at the Globe Theatre you will know what I mean.

It was a terrific thrill when I saw even the most determinedly beat, the most dedicated anti-deb, the most anti-fashion fanatic, taking to the new prettiness, for although it looks – and is meant to look – as sweet as sugar, it is sugar laced with the spice of sex appeal.

One day I pulled on an eight-year-old boy's sweater for fun. I was enchanted with the result. And, in six months, all the birds were wearing the skinny-ribs that resulted.

It was the same thing with string tops. As a joke, I put a man's string vest over the dark dress I was wearing. The effect was electric. I bought up all the string vests I could put my hands on and had them dyed in the colours of the year. Fashion became a thing of tangled textures and stringy shapes, of hole-peppered stockings, crochet tops and fishnet gloves. I loved the look.

To keep constantly in touch, Alexander and I watch all the young television programmes and we go to places like the Ad Lib where you can see the early signs of some new fad or craze beginning to develop amongst the most up and coming trend-setters. One night at the Ad Lib, there were seven girls wearing the same Ginger Group dress. And they all loved it. For me, it was confirmation that we're on the right track.

On the far side of the Atlantic, I had further confirmation. It came across to me when I was in New Orleans to receive the Rex Award given by Maison Blanche.

Once a year Maison Blanche give an Award to the top designer of each of the important European countries. We had a show to put on in New York around the same time and our idea was that after showing at Lord and Taylor, we would go on to New Orleans together. It didn't work out the way we'd planned.

The clothes we took out for Lord and Taylor got stuck in the customs … as usual. Alexander had to spend most of his time at the airport, hanging about there hour after hour, haggling with the officials and, finally, getting the men to work after hours to clear the stuff.

Lord and Taylor did all they could to help; it is one of the grandest stores in New York but, even so, the back door, well guarded by a posse of men with pistols on their hips, had to be kept open for us until two o'clock in the morning. We just managed to get the clothes inside the store in time and then Alexander and I had to unpack and hang them all up for the show next day.

We were booked to fly on to New Orleans in the afternoon but with all the hold-ups and delays, it was obviously impossible for us both to go.

I travelled with Sybil Connolly, Princess Galitzine and Crahay, the designer who used to be with Nina Ricci and is now with Lanvin.

There was a terrific party of V.I.P.s at the airport to see us off. A double line of pipers stretched from the lounge to the special jet which was taking us to New Orleans. When the embarkation order was given, all these pipers started blowing their heads off. I felt awful. I'd had no sleep. I felt lost amongst all these grandees without Alexander. I knew my face was getting pinker and pinker. My eyes misted over and I went tottering along between these terribly impressive-looking lines of pipers, stumbling up the steps of the plane in floods of tears.

We were only going to be separated for about a week so it probably all sounds rather ridiculous but I had looked forward to being in New Orleans with Alexander.

By luck Sybil Connolly sat beside me on the plane. She was marvellous. Obviously she grasped the situation at once. She kept up a straightforward, non-stop conversation while I sat there snivelling.

There was another terrific reception waiting for us at New Orleans. Once again the tarmac was double-lined with pipers from the plane to the lounge but this time the pipers were all girls, looking amazing in kilts and velvet jackets and little cocked hats. We were given an escort from the airport to our hotel with the police sounding off their sirens and all the rest of it.

Most of us were, in fact, dotty with exhaustion. Poor Sybil had flown all the way from Ireland ... she had been in the air something like sixteen hours ... but with all the difference in timing, this didn't mean a thing to our hosts. We went straight into a Press conference.

The next morning rehearsals started and went on solidly for two days.

Sybil and Crahay and Galitzine were showing terrific ball gowns and pretty dazzling clothes. It was a late night show – and very grand. Amongst all this, my very young dresses appeared out of place, particularly as most of the women in the audience were dowagers rather than teenagers and turned up in tiaras and minks and sables and that. Just about the whole town seems to put on full evening dress every night. New Orleans is about a hundred years behind the times. The audience that night was obviously puzzled, not only by my clothes but by the way they were shown.

Fortunately for me, Sybil Connolly had brought with her a marvellous model girl – Adrienne – who had a Vidal Sassoon haircut and who – it turned out – had bought some of my clothes at home. She was really with it; she understood what I'm after.

Sybil allowed Adrienne to show my things and to teach the other girls my way of showing. The audience gasped when these girls pranced down the catwalk. They'd never seen this kind of thing – or these kinds of clothes – before. But the next morning – Saturday – the newspapers were full of the show and it had obviously been a success.

Sybil and the others flew off back to New York but I had to stay on to pack up all our clothes and send these on to Montreal where I was to put on another show at Ogilvy's.

I went into Maison Blanche and found that my stuff (which of course had to be more highly priced there than it is in this country because of the import duties) had been put in the couture department. It was a seething mass of teenagers; there were between three and four hundred of them, all rushing about the place, snatching the garments off the rails and trying them on in any odd corner they could find. The staff, accustomed to the orderly stagnation of the couture department, were absolutely staggered. In desperation, the buyer asked me to stay and help with the selling.

I was besieged by these girls. They all had endless questions … what colour should be worn with what … which style should they choose … what did the girls in England wear for dances. It was terrifically exhilarating. These girls absolutely lapped up everything I was able to tell them. They said they had never had the chance before to meet and talk with a real live designer. They hadn't really believed such people existed. They thought of the whole fashion setup as an impersonal thing ... some huge Enterprise Inc., organized by people of the opposite sex who were much older anyway and produced the sort of thing they thought the young should wear and then went on to commercialize their ideas. They had never before had the chance to ask personal advice.

They even asked me how they should use their make-up. And this is important, for the interpretation of beauty changes just as clothes do.

What a great many people still don't realize is that the Look isn't just the garments you wear. It's the way you put your make-up on, the way you do your hair, the sort of stockings you choose, the way you walk and stand; even the way you smoke your fag. All these are a part of the same 'feeling'.

Make-up – old style – is out. It is used as expertly as ever but it is not designed to show. The ideal now is to look as though you have a baby skin untouched by cosmetics. Lipstick is kept to a pale gloss and the only area where you can go to town is round the eyes. There you can use the lot ... eyeshadow, eyeliner and lashings of mascara plus false eyelashes – even false eyebrows I should think – provided you've managed to master the art of putting them on and keeping them in place.

There was a time when every girl under twenty yearned to look like an experienced, sophisticated thirty; when round-faced teenagers practised sucking in their cheeks to achieve interesting hollows; when every girl dreamed of a slinky black dress worn with very high heels.

All this is in reverse with a vengeance now. Suddenly, every girl with a hope of getting away with it is aiming to look not only under voting age but under the age of consent. The merest hint of interesting hollows has them doubling up on their daily pinta and their ambition is to look like Patty Boyd rather than Marlene Dietrich. Their aim is to look childishly young, naïvely unsophisticated. And it takes more sophistication to work out the Look than those earlier would be sophisticates ever dreamed of.

When I did finally get away from the department, I had to get all the clothes I'd brought over for the show checked and packed and down to the airport. Alexander had given me a whole sheaf of instructions about what I had to do and what I had not got to do and I was practically demented going through all these notes and double-checking that I hadn't slipped up on a thing. I had this awful 'in bond' thing hanging over my head and the memory of the ghastly time Alexander had had at Kennedy Airport less than a week before.

I stayed until all the clothes were packed and correctly labelled and went down to the airport with them. I made sure – I thought – that it would be absolutely impossible for anything to go wrong.

Then I stumbled back to the hotel, completely worn out and miserable because, in spite of being in the place four days, I hadn't seen a thing I really wanted to see. We'd been so fêted and looked after; we'd been given a marvellous time and masses of the most delicious food. But I had had no time to go off and explore the places and things I really wanted to explore.

It was a terribly hot night. The temperature in New Orleans was between eighty and ninety at breakfast and from then on went up steadily to well over a hundred in the middle of the day. It was dark by eight o'clock but the temperature was still in the eighties.

I went up to the roof of the hotel where there's a swimming pool to have a drink and try to cool down and somehow or other I drifted into conversation with the only other person up there on his own. This man turned out to be a New York lawyer who was in New Orleans for just a few days, as I was. He had just completed the negotiations for some terrific multi-million-dollar merger and was having his first quiet breath of air after days in a conference room.

When we'd had a drink we decided the only thing to do was to go for a swim. This made us feel so much better that it seemed quite crazy to go to bed and leave in the morning without ever having seen anything of the town.

That night I really saw something of the old New Orleans. The French quarter of the town is absolutely wild ... full of mad bars with jazz pouring out of every one of them ... just as I had always imagined it would be. And, intermingled with these bars, there are the most incredible do-it-yourself sex shops with the most extraordinary contraptions in the windows ... lights that go up and out ... whistles that go off ... bells that ring ... odd-looking tassels ... and the most peculiar electrical equipment of all kinds. If anything like one of these shops opened in this country it would be closed by the police within ten minutes.

As we walked down the streets we could look into the bars and see the strip-tease acts going on. The performances are always on top of the bar so that passers-by see a certain amount and can't resist going in for more. It's fantastic strip-tease ... wilder than anything I've ever imagined. And all the time there is this terrific jazz beating out. Just as when you walk down Bond Street it seems as if every shop is a shoe shop, so in the French quarter of New Orleans it seems as if every place is a strip-tease jazz bar. And the jazz is terrific. The players get so excited that they do a sort of strip-tease of their own. The tie comes off first, then the jacket, then the shirt ... and all the time the music never stops. It gets louder and louder and louder and more and more frenzied. Sometimes a player will become almost epileptic and have to be held down by others. The whole crowd – players and audience – get so wild that they all mingle together and then pour out into the street ... a mad shindy of people following some modern Pied Piper in what appears to be a wild tribal dance.

It is an extraordinary place. Nobody appears to eat until midnight and nobody thinks of going to bed till the early hours. Drinking starts at about six so by the time dinner comes round nearly everyone is more or less stoned. I simply couldn't stand up to all this hard drinking and no eating until midnight. I had to change my entire eating routine. I never had any lunch but I'd make sure I had something like a club sandwich at the hotel about six before I had a drink.

Our night on the town finished up around five in the morning. I had to leave the hotel at six to be at the airport at seven to catch the plane to New York which connected with the plane to Montreal I was expected on. I didn't go to bed at all. I was thankful I hadn't got to bother any more about the clothes. I had done everything

Alexander had told me to do and I was quite sure these were already safely on their way.

I fell asleep the moment I was on board the plane, happy that I hadn't missed out on New Orleans altogether and completely confident that I'd find the trunk waiting for me in New York and would only have to get it put on the plane to Montreal. I had about twenty minutes between planes to do this and I had Alexander's list of instructions to help me. According to this, all I had to do was hand the keys to customs, get the trunk cleared and see it on the plane.

It sounded easy. It should have been easy. But, of course, when I got there, the trunk could not be found. At first, I refused to believe it. It simply had to be there. I'd practically put it on the plane from New Orleans myself. Masses of telephone calls were made all over the place but there wasn't a trace. Somehow, between New Orleans and New York, the trunk had evaporated. Nobody knew a thing about it. We didn't see it again until some weeks later when it finally turned up at London Airport.

Of course I missed my flight and had to wait a couple of hours before I could get a seat on another one. I was worried stiff; the only thing to do was to have a drink.

Then I discovered that the only money I had on me was a hundred dollar note. Nobody in the bar had sufficient change. 'Try the restaurant,' the barman said. I went to the restaurant. It was too early in the morning for there to be much money in the till there.

'Try the main desk,' the restaurant manager said. I went to the main desk. They didn't have that kind of money lying around.

Everything seemed to be piling up against me. I stumbled round the airport, going from one place to the next. I couldn't find anyone who could change that hundred dollar bill. The very fact that I couldn't buy a drink made me want it more. And I discovered that I was starving!

I staggered back into the bar where I'd started. At least it would be somewhere to sit. I found that the news had got round that some bird was going round hopelessly trying to change a hundred dollar bill and some people, buying a round, had seen the funny side of the whole thing and had bought an extra one for me! There was a whole row of drinks on the counter waiting for me!

When I did finally board the plane I was completely cut and rather thankfully so because I simply couldn't bear to face up to the predicament I was in … an enormous lunch in my honour the next day and no clothes to show. On top of all this, I realized I was not on the plane I was expected on; I had completely forgotten the name of the store promoting my designs; I couldn't remember the name of the President or of the buyer; and I hadn't the faintest idea of the name of the hotel where I was supposed to be staying.

I just had to hope that someone would think of meeting every plane in from New York that day knowing that I must eventually turn up.

When we arrived at Montreal, there was a hurricane blowing. I had left New Orleans just a few hours earlier in a temperature between eighty and ninety and here I was, dressed in a thin crêpe dress, in a real old hurricane with a howling wind and rain and snow.

Hoping against hope, I looked round the airport to see if anyone was there to meet me. No one took the slightest interest in my arrival. I sat on my suitcase and waited; there was nothing else I could do.

Hours went by. I just sat there waiting. Suddenly the name of the store came to me. I dashed to the telephone. I was too late. The store had closed for the night and there was no one there to answer the phone.

I went back to my suitcase. Cleaners appeared with buckets and mops. I was in their way but I was too tired and cold and hopeless to do anything about it. My feet were frozen. The wind never stopped howling. I kept telling myself that sometime or other someone must turn up to look for me. But time went on.

Suddenly a very distraught-looking young man dashed in and he came over and said, 'Are you her?'

I said, 'Well, yes … I suppose I am.'

'God, how glad I am to find you,' he went on. 'I'm terribly late. I thought you'd have gone.'

He was so distraught and I was so distraught that this kind of crazy conversation went on.

'You can imagine how I've been feeling,' he said. 'I didn't know your name or anything. My boss was going to come and meet you himself but he's had some sort of domestic crisis and he couldn't make it. He just dashed into the office and screamed at me, "Go to the airport and find her. Quick. Get going. Get on with it." He was in such a state that I didn't stop to ask questions.'

We went on talking in this hopeless way. We weren't able to clue up on anything. But I did eventually discover that he certainly hadn't come from Ogilvy's. I wasn't the 'her' he was looking for.

He offered to drive me into Montreal and take me to an hotel. It seemed the only sensible thing to do now. I was just about to get up from my suitcase and leave with him when we heard a terrific din behind the customs and the sound of shouting. Then the doors into the lounge shot open and a frightfully elegant but extremely distraught woman, wearing a most impressive hat, came in followed by three or four photographers. She didn't seem to notice me which was not surprising since, sitting on my suitcase as I was, I certainly couldn't have looked anything like a fashion designer. But one of the cameramen must have seen a photograph and recognized me. He dashed over and started taking pictures. By the time this woman realized what was happening, he had got his pictures. She was frightfully angry because these weren't the sort of photographs she wanted at all but it was too late. They were in all the papers the following day. Instead of the grand arrival everyone expected to see, there was one frozen-to-death face peering disconsolately up from a rather battered suitcase in an empty airport.

Poor woman! I was terribly sorry for her. She had been told Alexander would be with me. That's why she hadn't recognized me. She drove me into Montreal and I found the largest suite in the very grand Ritz Hotel had been booked for us. Practically the whole of the store were there to welcome me even though it was so late and they had been waiting so long. I rather suspect now that they were really waiting so that they could have a private view of the suite I had been given. I discovered I had the rooms Liz Taylor and Richard Burton had on their wedding night. I was a good excuse! People poured in and out the rest of the evening.

It was an enormous suite … to me rather like a palace … fantastic. There was a vast bed, the biggest I've ever seen. I thought ours at home was king-size till I saw this one. And there was a huge kitchen full of every kind of drink.

Strangely I felt quite at home there in spite of all the grandeur. It was all so relaxed and friendly and cosy after New York and New Orleans. The schedule I was given was totally unlike the high-powered kind of operation one has to contend with in America. And when I was finally able to get ready for bed, I found the same sort of crazy things one is apt to find at home. All the dozens of lamps in this vast suite had to be turned off separately … there was no master switch to deal with the lot. And the five telephones all had separate numbers so they could all ring at once. It took me between three and four hours to get dressed in the morning because the moment I turned on the shower one phone would go and before I'd finished, another would be ringing. I spent my time dashing from one to the other, trying hopelessly to trace the one that was ringing.

The show was supposed to go on at lunch time that day. All the fashion writers of Montreal, as well as vast numbers from other bits of Canada, had been invited. I telephoned the airport at six in the morning but there was no news of the trunk. I had to face up to the fact that I had nothing to show.

Two model girls had been booked by the store and by absolute luck one of them turned out to be exactly my size. She had a Vidal's sort of haircut, too! The only thing I could do was to ask this girl to wear my own personal things … the clothes I had brought with me to wear myself.

She put these on and trotted about while I talked like mad trying to distract the guests and give them something to write about. I don't think I have ever talked so long or so hard. Everyone was so sorry for me that in the end the whole thing went off quite well.

Some of the journalists were rather distant at first but they liked the few clothes we were able to show and finally there seemed to be a sort of Dunkirk spirit about the whole thing. In fact, at the end, one journalist got up and proposed a toast ... all very emotional and rather sentimental ... on the lines of something like so long as there are people like Mary Quant there'll always be an England. I was terribly touched. It was a wonderful ending to what might very well have been a ghastly experience.

And I actually got back to London Airport on the plane I was originally booked on. Alexander was there to meet me. He didn't really expect me because he'd got wind that everything was going wrong. He'd come to the airport just in case. And he couldn't believe it when he saw me coming off the plane!

It was soon after these adventures that I got my first chance to design foundation garments. It's exciting work. Underwear should be an integral part of the current look; most often, it's not.

I know I am always seduced myself by the prettiest, frilliest, laciest bras that look so good when you're half undressed. But, under a dress, they are nothing but unsightly bumps and lumps.

I refuse to accept a suspender that disfigures the clothes that go over it. I simply hate suspenders. To me, they look like some sort of fearful surgical device. There must be dozens of ways of keeping stockings up more attractively and just as effectively. I said this on television once and I was swamped with all kinds of strange Heath Robinson devices. I'd like to think that one day all suspenders will be flat and pretty, something like jewels, and invisible under the flimsiest dress.

I can't see any reason why foundation garments should not be sleek and modern and pretty and fit and move with the body at the same time. Women don't want to have to be fitted. They hate the idea of some other woman fiddling round with their bra. I can remember walking out of a shop in Knightsbridge where I was trying to buy a new foundation simply because the assistant would insist on coming into the dressing room with me. This kind of thing is all too embarrassing.

And foundations should be inexpensive. We have this obsession about washing so obviously they are not going to last for ever. Personally I think this hygiene business can be overdone. I have noticed that the people in the spotless countries are less welcoming, more inhibited, than those in countries where they are not so fussy. The north of France, for instance, is cleaner but far less fun than the south.

I think we've progressed quite a way in our outlook in the past few years but we haven't made it yet. I would like to plunge in and try to change the whole conception in one swoop. But it wouldn't work. In a commercial world, you can't change too much too quickly. Production lines are not geared for it; anyway, there are always a lot of people who are shocked. I have learned now to move forward gingerly in the direction I want to go.

When I first had to get the manufacturers to accept my ideas on the way I think foundation garments should be shown I had to be pretty crafty. I knew they wanted me to use the usual underwear models ... a bevy of very well-upholstered, early-middle-aged ladies. I was horrified and quite terrified that the Press would see my garments for the first time in this way. Not even the great couturiers would show designs made specially for the larger-than-normal middle-aged on a larger-than-normal middle-aged model. I worried about it for days. I didn't really want to have an open battle about it.

Eventually I managed to persuade the manufacturers to let me choose the girls; then I had to persuade the girls to do the show for me. A lot of them are friends of mine and I know they'll do anything they can to help but I had to persuade their agencies too. And agencies don't like their best girls to show underwear.

Finally Jan de Souza, our staff model at the Ginger Group showroom in South Molton Street, came to my rescue and proved my point. One afternoon I dashed her round to the Youthlines place so they could see what I meant about the type of girl who should show foundations.

The Chairman and his fellow directors sat around while Jan showed my new designs, swinging down the catwalk in her usual rangy way. There was complete silence in the room. The atmosphere was electric. No one there had ever seen any other but the old-fashioned type of corsetry model mincing rather coyly up and down. And here was Jan looking absolutely fantastic. They simply goggled; they couldn't believe it.

Jan – who is quite unaware of her beautiful body – had no idea what it was all about. She didn't notice a thing. As soon as we finished, I simply shot her out of the place and that was that. I knew by that time that provided I was able to get girls like Jan to show, I would be allowed to go ahead in my own way.

When the first Press show was over, even Alexander said it was the most erotic thing he had ever seen in his life. He is accustomed to lounging around in the cabine with the girls in various stages of undress but for the first time, he says, he became conscious that he'd better be careful which way he was looking!

We had just got the foundation designing well under way when we had another surprise telephone call. This time it was from America ... from a man who announced himself as Carl Rosen, President of Puritan Fashions. He said he was coming over to England the next day and would like to see what we were doing.

Alexander wasn't awfully enthusiastic. We had had a lot of American manufacturers making overtures to us by this time and he said, 'I'm sorry, but I don't think we know anything about you. We've never heard of you.' This was a pity because Puritan are one of the three biggest manufacturers in the States.

Some twelve hours later, at the crack of dawn, we had another call from Carl. He was at Claridge's. He said, 'Can you lend me someone to show me round London? I am very interested in the whole young thing here and I'd like to see everything that's going on.'

Alexander felt we had perhaps been rather offhand and we ought to make some sort of gesture. He rang up Annabel, his assistant and buyer for the Bazaar shops, and asked her to go along to Claridge's. She had breakfast with Carl there and spent the whole day taking him round. She took him everywhere and made sure he saw all our rivals were doing.

The next day Alexander and I lunched with him at the Connaught. We found him to be the most elegant and civilized dress manufacturer we had ever met. He is one of the most riveting men we know.

He said, 'Supposing I wanted to produce a Mary Quant line in the States and put it over in a really big way, would you be interested?'

We said, 'Yes. But we must tell you first about our contract with Penney's.'

We told him how we first met Penney's through Paul Young and Bob Pegna; of the enormous sums of money they had paid us and were still paying us; and of our own feeling that no department store in the States would touch my things now that my name was so closely tied up with the J. C. Penney chain.

Carl said he didn't think this would matter too much to his company as they concentrated on supplying such a very different market. When we parted, he said he would be in touch again.

We really didn't think anything would come of it.

Carl went back to America and soon afterwards, by one of those curious coincidences, he met Paul Young. Probably because they were both in the garment business and Carl had met us in London so recently, my name came up. And of course Paul knew all about us and what we had been doing. I suppose he gave a pretty enthusiastic account of all that was going on in London and said what a tremendously international fashion centre this City has become. He must have enthused about all the young designers he has met over here. Obviously Carl was intrigued, not only by what Paul said, but by Paul himself. I think he probably made up his mind at that meeting that he must have Paul working with him in his company and that he would go ahead with his plans for marketing my designs.

This was a big step forward for an American manufacturer. Over there, until now, these people have never promoted any individual designer on a long-term basis. Their theory has been that to build a business on any 'name' personality is far too risky. He – or she – may be run over by a bus or drop dead or clear off with someone else and a huge business, in which millions of dollars may well have been invested, will simply disappear overnight.

In this country the importance of design in mass production has begun to be recognized but it is still hard for many manufacturers to accept the fact that although design may not be the most important part of the operation, it must come first.

The days when someone in a manufacturer's workroom produced a garment which had had some success the previous season and said, 'We've done pretty well with this … let's run it again' have gone for ever.

The three essentials of well co-ordinated fashion … design, manufacture and distribution … have got to run together or you are left with nothing.

The difficulty, from a manufacturer's point of view, is to recognize the young designer of real talent before she disappears, pushed under by the struggle for survival. It isn't easy. Creative ability is not the only quality essential to success.

A designer has got to be able to keep her feet well and solidly on the ground if she is going to be tuned in to the fast-moving changes of fashion. She has got to be able to get up when the alarm clock goes off … and that's far too early for anyone in their right mind … get to the workrooms on time … deal with all sorts of creative and emotional people with different problems, different temperaments … encourage the downhearted … enthuse the lazy … see cloth from all over the world … make quick decisions which may well involve thousands of pounds … talk incessantly on the telephone … visit mills and factories to keep in touch with what's new … and, at the end of all this, find some quiet corner where she can get down to her real work and produce designs to a deadline.

This last – for me – represents hours of agony … of doing hundreds of sketches till I get to the one that begins to look like what I'm after … of existing on endless cups of black coffee and corn-flakes … of sleepless nights if I ever manage to get to bed at all. It is absolute hell at first and it is only when I am beginning to come to the end of a collection that I discover it's all been rather fun and I'm enjoying myself.

I think the potential quality of a new young designer can be recognized by several things. His – or her – passionate belief in what he is doing; endless enthusiasm; a deep conviction that what he wants to achieve, he will achieve; limitless imagination; a capacity for hard work; physical strength; a tolerant personality; and an instinctive sense of timing.

Creative talent on its own is just not enough. To be able to work with other people is terribly important; so is the ability to adapt an idea for mass production without losing 'the look'. A 'look' can so easily become weak and diluted and disintegrated when garments have to be made in all sizes for all types. I have seen it slaughtered in mass production.

Out of all these qualities it is probably the first – the passionate belief – that can be the most exhausting from a manufacturer's viewpoint. But – to me – it is the most easily recognizable of them all. It is the difference between one who really cares and one who is quite content if his name appears in the papers often enough.

The designer who will choose a deliberate gimmick simply to get a splash in the Press is likely to have a short-term success. But it can only be 'a flash in the pan'. It can't last. No dedicated designer will ever produce anything simply as a gimmick though it is quite possible that a genuine and sincere idea may be interpreted as gimmicky at first.

Changes in fashion have seldom been accepted immediately without derision. But if the original design is good and exciting and true to trend then – however outrageous it may at first appear – it will succeed. It will be a legitimate indication of the direction in which fashion is moving forward even though a season or two may have to go by before it can be fully appreciated and accepted everywhere. This is one of the risks which manufacturers, once they have decided to back a young designer, must recognize and accept.

In my own case, things like black boots, black stockings, embroidered and patterned stockings, pinafore and high-waisted dresses were all labelled 'gimmicks' when they first appeared but some of them stuck and they became an integral part of the advance of fashion. The thing is that the true, dedicated designer is more likely to be right than anybody else. Even her mistakes will prove something. She will have a flair for introducing something new at the moment when people are unconsciously wanting a change.

In past years, pacemakers have usually been foreign. Chanel gave us the cardigan suit; Dior the 'new look'; Pucci put the rich into silk shirts. But today some of the pace-setting news comes from Britain.

All this is something of which a man like Carl Rosen is fully aware. The gamble he is taking is carefully considered. In his plans to pioneer a new world of Youthquake fashion in the States, he is signing up other young designers ... British, French and American ... as well as us.

To finalize his plans for the introduction of this new idea, we lived through weeks of the most fantastic negotiations. Before the contracts we had to sign were completed and exchanged, Alexander had to go over to the States four times; I went with him twice and Carl came over here three times. All this in the course of three months.

On his first visit, Alexander went to see the Penney people to let them know what was going on. He called at their new forty-six-storey building in New York to see the Vice-President most closely connected with our contract. He had no qualms about this because we all felt the arrangement we planned to make with Puritan – who would distribute only in top department stores of which there are literally thousands coast to coast, and had agreed to spend huge sums of money promoting my name – must react to the advantage of Penney's who were selling other designs of mine at far cheaper prices and in quite a different market. Apart from anything else, we felt they must benefit from the wider promotion of the Mary Quant name.

Unfortunately, Penney's didn't see the thing as we did and poor Alexander had to argue for hours although he could hardly concentrate at all because of two men with paper wings pinned between their shoulder-blades washing the windows of the Vice-President's suite above the clouds of New York.

Penney's had to be convinced because – apart from the truth of the matter that they would benefit from our prestige expansion – it is essential that the people one works for are aware of one's integrity and know that they get good value from the designs they buy. Finally Penney's came to and realized what a good thing our new deal was for them. They offered us a new, three-year, contract!

Meantime, the deal with Puritan had been on ... off ... on ... off. And in spite of all these It's on! ... It's off! ... patches, I had to go on designing the collection because I knew that if contracts were finalized we would be up against time.

During one of our 'It's on' periods, when it seemed that the deal had been agreed in principle although there were still all sorts of qualifications and complications to be sorted out, we gave a dinner party for Carl in London.

We asked about twenty-five people to meet him and took over most of a restaurant called La Popote which is run by friends of ours and is rather the same sort of place as Alexander's used to be.

Rudolf Nureyev sat next to Carl. I suppose they were never properly introduced or, if they were, Carl just didn't register. After about an hour, he turned to Nureyev and said, 'What do you do?'

Nureyev got up and walked out. Others in the party who are particular friends of his rushed after him. Somehow they managed to calm him down and persuade him to come back.

While all this was going on Carl said to Alexander, 'What the hell did I say?'

Alexander said, 'That's Nureyev.'

'Who's he?'

When Nureyev came back, Carl turned to him at once.

'I must apologize,' he said, 'I didn't hear your name. I should have recognized you. Every time you're in New York I catch every single performance you give. I think you are the most fabulous dancer in the world. I've seen nearly all the great dancers in my time. You're the greatest of them all.'

He simply charmed Nureyev back into a good mood. They struck up a tremendous friendly thing.

Sitting opposite Carl at the dinner table was Terry Hooper and his brand-new wife, Pru. Terry was working pretty successfully at one of the best private gaming clubs in London and making a lot of money but he was rather fed-up with the hours he had to keep. When Carl said to him, 'What do you do?' Terry told him.

Carl said, 'It seems to me that you should be a pretty good salesman.'

And Terry replied that he thought he was quite good.

Then Carl said, 'Do you think you would like to work in New York on Mary's clothes?'

'Yes, I would.'

'Can you come tomorrow?'

Terry thought it was a joke and said, 'Yes.'

'Right,' Carl said. 'I'll fix your tickets.'

It was as quick and unexpected as that!

Then Carl turned to me and asked me how much he would have to pay Terry. The next few minutes were quite frantic. A sort of auction took place. I was frightfully worried and embarrassed about the whole thing and the awful responsibility being put on me. I didn't want to commit myself … or Terry and Pru.

When Carl suggested a figure, I just said, 'Well … w-e-l-l.' I was petrified for Terry. Fortunately Carl kept on putting the price up gradually while I went on in this noncommittal way. Finally he reached what I thought a very reasonable figure indeed. Then he went back slightly. I snapped in quickly and made it a deal.

That was it. A few days later Terry and Pru took off for New York. In those few days they sold off everything … they got rid of their flat, sold the car and lived in their parents' clothes so that everything they possessed could be cleaned before they went. They gave a farewell dinner party every night, each time for the same people, and worked themselves into a terrific state of frantic anxiety. Their friends were well fed but emotionally exhausted.

Alexander managed to be in New York ahead of them. He went to Kennedy to meet them. This was awfully important because it really was the most tremendous step for them to take. Neither of them knew anything of America and they had burnt their boats over here. It was the most climactic time for them, specially for Pru who had been married only a week and had to say good-bye to her parents.

When Alexander saw them walking through the customs it was obvious that they were both exhausted. Their faces were absolutely grey. Pru looked a little tearful. They looked lost. Pru was homesick. She kept saying she must phone her mother.

Fortunately Carl had lent Alexander one of his cars to go to the airport. Billy, the driver, noticed how wretched Pru looked and heard her say how much she wanted to speak to her mother. He turned round and asked, 'What's your mother's number?' And Pru, thinking he was just asking out of interest, told him.

Alexander saw Billy fiddling round with some knobs on the dashboard but he really had no idea of what was going on. In a couple of minutes, Billy handed Pru the radio telephone.

'There you are, Mrs Hooper,' he said. 'I have your mother on the line.'

This was too much for Pru who burst into tears.

Alexander went with them to the Hilton, saw them settled in, then had to dash back to the airport to catch the London plane. He thought every single detail of the deal with Puritan had at last been agreed and finalized and when he walked into the flat, the first thing he said to me was, 'Do you know what you are, you bitch? You're a millionaire!' Only a dollar millionaire of course, and only in theory, but better than a poke in the eye with a dirty stick.

But there were more problems to come. Complications kept cropping up till the last minute. Archie and Alexander had made up their minds that I was not going to be allowed to take the collection I had made for Puritan out of this country until absolutely every single detail had been agreed. We had spent thousands of pounds on the negotiations that had already taken place, and on getting a collection together. We were not going to spend a penny more until everything was signed, sealed and delivered. I realized later – when I learned a little of the way the fashion business goes over there from personal experience – how right they were!

I had about sixty designs ready for Puritan ... dresses and sportswear. The patterns were cut. Everything was ready to go. But still there was one delay after another.

The negotiations were so complicated and so drawn out that finally we actually missed the plane we were supposed to travel in. We were on the phone all that night when we should have been in the air. The calls were flying back and forth between the New York lawyers and us. Alexander simply would not compromise. He insisted that I could not – and would not – bring out the collection until we had a really solid basis for the business we all hoped was to develop. Finally Carl came on the line and Alexander switched on his secret, sneaky little recording machine.

'O.K.,' said Carl. 'This is the letter I posted today ... is your machine working? I will read it to you.'

It turned out that we had the tape in the wrong way round anyway and so ... nonplussed and exhausted ... we caught the milk plane from London Airport.

With all the red tape involved when one is trying to send original designs and garments out of this country, it was impossible for us to send the collection in the orthodox 'in bond' way. We were so short of time with these last-minute negotiations that we simply dared not risk it. I had to be back in London in five days and there was a lot of work to be done on the designs in New York before these could go into mass production. We've had plenty of experience of the kind of thing that can happen. The customs people might well decide to hold up the consignment for three or four days. This has happened to us in both France and America, and on one earlier trip to the States all the gear eventually arrived practically knee-deep in water and absolutely ruined.

In the old days we would probably have bundled everything into a clutter of cardboard boxes and borrowed crates but we felt this wasn't the sort of thing expected of us now. Alexander rushed out and bought nine expensive-looking crocodile cases.

We decided the only thing was to arrive looking like two immensely rich, slightly dotty people who crossed the world for a few days' holiday with nine suitcases full of brand-new clothes.

We had these sixty dresses with us as well as some of my own personal things. We kept on reassuring each other that there are people who do travel with fantastic amounts of luggage and that we did not look nearly so extraordinary as we thought. So far as Alexander was concerned, it needed a great deal of reassurance. Alexander has always had a great thing about travelling light. He likes to walk out of one country and into another on the other side of the world with a paper bag containing a razor and toothbrush. It's a fantasy thing of his ... something to do with having editions of everything he owns in London, Paris, New York and Tokyo ... which he doesn't!

We arrived at Kennedy. We knew it was going to be a bit difficult to swing those nine crocodile cases. While Alexander was waiting for them to be unloaded, I walked up and down the customs part, sweltering in my eccentric fur coat, trying to look the way I imagined an extremely rich and pampered tourist might look and hoping to spot a likely looking official who might be sympathetic to a dotty woman visiting New York for four days with nine suitcases. I saw one who looked Italian ... I felt he might be my man. And he was! He didn't seem the least surprised that I should travel with so many clothes.

The first thing we had to do was to put on a presentation of the garments to all the heads of the Puritan empire ... about forty of them. None of these people had ever seen my clothes before. They knew nothing of the London Look and what we were trying to do. Only Carl and Paul Young were prepared for what they were going to see. We had to enthuse all the others. At one stage Paul mentioned Courrèges and they had not heard of him either so I cheered up!

I found some American models had been engaged for my show ... rather big bosomed types ... not exactly my idea of the model girl shape ... but very professional and sexy by American standards.

Fortunately all went well. The clothes stood up to the critical examination they were given and everyone was tremendously excited. Then there was a great squabble amongst all the heads of the different departments about who was going to have this and who would take that. 'Departments' are really subsidiary companies and there is intense rivalry between them.

Carl stands aside from these fireworks. He plays his usual game of leaving his executives to make their own decisions and fight it out amongst themselves.

Eventually they came to some sort of agreement. Someone said in a loud voice, 'Right! Let's go!' And immediately everybody dispersed, dashing out of the room and shouting a great deal.

I was given the executives' conference room as my 'office'. I was told that I had to decide from which American firms I would be able to get the materials I wanted. All these firms had already been alerted. There were about sixty salesmen waiting outside the door, all loaded with armfuls of fabrics and huge books of swatches.

My job was to see them all; choose the cloth that would be right for the garments I had designed and give the orders. There are always various slight alterations to be made in another country; for instance, the American market demands a cloth of lighter weight than we use here and there are certain things like my favourite button cuffs that they say won't sell (though they will probably be all the rage next year). I was quite prepared to adapt my patterns slightly to conform to such things as these but I was determined we were going to keep the Look. Fortunately my experience with Penney's and Steinberg's has taught me a lot. I understand pretty well now when it is going to be worth while making a scene and when I've just got to accept.

While all this was going on Alexander rushed about visiting the fashion journalists and the Butterick paper pattern people and looking for a company to make my underwear for America. I had just completed my fourth collection for Butterick. We have had a great success with these. Some of our colleagues – perhaps I should say competitors though I don't think of them that way – are having the same sort of success. The Butterick people consider that a big seller is one that goes up to 30,000 patterns and we know that several of mine have hit the 70,000 mark. According to Russ Norris, the very bright young man who first contacted us on this project, this is terrific. In the editions in which my designs have been featured, they have been the bestsellers; in other editions, when Jean Muir or Gerald McCann have appeared, they, too, have produced the best-sellers.

There was so much we wanted to do in the four days we were in New York that the only way to get through it all was for Alexander to deal with all these things while I concentrated on the Puritan collections.

I was fully prepared for hard work but I really had no idea just how hard it was going to be. I have never seen people work as Carl and his staff do. They start at eight-thirty in the morning and work right through the day. They don't stop for lunch; they get coffee out of the coffee machine in the building and send out for doughnuts when they must eat. They finish about seven-thirty.

Carl works on the principle of finding the right person for the job, paying them too much, working them hard, and looking after them well. If he thinks one of his staff is looking tired after a particularly gruelling week, he thinks nothing of sending this man and his family to Florida for the week-end in a private plane. He's tough; but he is generous, too.

He himself rushes about so much that he never has time to be fitted for his suits. Fortunately one of his executives is very much the same height and size. Carl's clothes are all fitted on this man who – according to Carl – is just waiting for him to drop dead so that he can inherit the wardrobe.

I had a close-up of the way these people work that first day at the Puritan building. From the moment I heard those words … 'Right! Let's go!' … it never stopped.

The salesmen waiting to see me with their samples of cloth were allowed into the room one at a time at three-minute intervals. All these men were in competition with each other and fighting for orders. They jostled and pushed each other all over the place. The moment one of them was in, he'd say, 'Hi, Mary!' as if he'd known me all his life. It was a bit overwhelming at first and I suppose I showed something of what I was feeling in my face. Then I had such remarks as, 'I see … new designer … here today … gone tomorrow' thrown at me. And it was said with real bitterness. It shook me.

The whole setup was like a bedlam market to me till I got used to it. When I did settle down, I was enormously impressed. So far as the cloth manufacturers are concerned, America is certainly switched on.

When I saw a cloth I wanted, I would say, 'Right. I'll buy that one. How quickly can we have it?'

'I'll bring it right back.'

And the salesman literally ran out of the door. Ten minutes later, he was back with the length of cloth I had ordered.

It was unbelievable. In England I would have had to wait months.

There was one particular fabric I'd set my heart on for one of my designs. I couldn't find it over there but one man produced something very like it. The salesman saw I was interested but I told him I would have to go on searching because it wasn't exactly what I was looking for.

'We can make it for you,' he said.

'Yes, I'm sure you can. But there's no time.'

'We can make it for you *now*.'

'There isn't time,' I repeated.

'But I'm in the building next door,' he screamed back at me. 'Come and I'll show you.'

I told him I had another appointment in a few minutes but he persisted. 'Come with me. It's just next door.'

He was so insistent that I went. I did not realize what 'next door' means in New York. Going down in the lift feels like the first three miles ... 'next door' means the next block and that seems like another half mile ... then there's another lift to take you up yet another three miles.

However, we finally arrived. Obviously the firm was just moving in; there were decorators and painters all over the place. I was hurried into a back room and saw there a miniature weaving loom with stacks of spools of different coloured threads all round the walls. We sat down and, between us, this man and I worked out the design I wanted. In two hours, the length of material made to my design was handed to me. I had nine yards of it. In another two hours I saw the finished garment.

I had never imagined that work could be done at such speed. But it was tough. Those four days in New York are probably the toughest I have ever lived through to date. I had probably been to New York about fifteen times in recent years and enjoyed every one of my visits. This time I began to hate it. I couldn't bear all these salesmen besieging me every hour of the day. I felt I was being mobbed. The dress manufacturing industry in America is simply terrifying.

The second day I was working at Puritan, I arrived promptly at eight-thirty like the rest of the staff. 1400 Broadway is one of the three main buildings around which the whole of the ready-to-wear garment trade of New York centres. It is about thirty storeys high and it is entirely occupied by firms producing the same sort of garments. It is like Oxford Street set on end and poking straight up into the sky.

As I walked in, I was just one of hundreds of people pouring into the place. I wasn't at all sure which lift I ought to get in and everyone was in such a hurry I was pushed all over the place. Finally I was practically forced into one by a whole lot of people shoving from behind. Everyone started to call out the floor number they wanted ... twenty-two ... fourteen ... twelve ... eighteen. I wanted the fourth floor so, very nervously, I said quietly, 'Four, please.'

No one took the slightest notice. Twenty-two ... fourteen ... twelve ... and so on and on. I really was rather scared of getting lost so even more timidly I said again, 'Four, please.'

This time a female voice from the back of the lift took command. 'Who does she think she is? Only been in the building one day. Thinks she owns the place.'

I dared not open my mouth again. Suddenly it hit me. I understood the way these people were thinking. I was an English girl in New York taking over a job that they felt should have gone to an American. I was competition. And I was fair game. It was the same sensation as when I heard those salesmen say, 'new designer ... here today ... gone tomorrow'.

I went up to the top and when everyone else had got out of the lift, I came down to the fourth floor again.

I had a tough day. I suppose I met another two to three hundred people. I hadn't the slightest idea who any of them were. The clothes were hanging on rails in the room I worked in. And all the time there were people rushing in and out. I had no way of knowing who they were. I kept seeing garments taken off the rails and disappearing. A man would dash in, say 'Hi, Mary', grab a few dresses and make off. I even gave the patterns to some of them.

It was too late when I discovered that some of them were competitors. Everyone in the building knew what was going on at Puritan and rival firms were madly keen to see what I was up to. Before we left New York, Alexander and I saw one of my new designs on sale in the shops. And the dresses had not been made by Puritan.

That night it was about seven o'clock when I finished all I had to do. The building was practically empty but it was still light. I looked for a cab but at this time of day on Broadway it is practically impossible to get one. I decided I might just as well walk to the Algonquin. I was just starting off when one of the Puritan chaps came up behind me and said he would try and get me a cab. It was hopeless.

'I'll walk,' I said.

'You can't do that,' he said. He looked quite shocked at the idea. 'You can't ... you certainly can't walk up 39th Street alone.'

He wasn't supposed to be responsible for my welfare so far as Puritan were concerned and I couldn't understand what he was getting at.

I started off and he trotted along beside me. Fortunately, half-way up 39th we managed to get a cab.

Afterwards Alexander and I were told that a girl from the building had been chased up 39th and murdered only a few days before. She was stabbed forty times. The street was full of people just as it was the night I was there and not a single person had done a thing to help. Nobody got the police. They just walked past. They didn't want to be involved.

Even though I didn't know this at the time, I was pretty thankful when I reached the Algonquin. Alexander and I love this place. It's where we always stay. We don't feel so homesick there. It's a bit old-fashioned and not at all the general conception of a super glossy American hotel. The great thing is that from the moment we arrived there on our second visit we've been treated like old friends and even if this isn't true, it's awfully nice just the same. It is also convenient. It is near Broadway and the hive of the garment industry and right next door to Fifth Avenue.

Nothing at the Algonquin ever appears to change. We are the ones who change. When we first stayed there we'd take the bus from the airport. Now we turn up in a tremendous limousine laid on by Carl. In the last few months I've been turning up there pretty frequently, sometimes with Alexander or Archie, more often without them.

I was so nervous about the way they might treat my designs that at one time I was virtually a weekly commuter between London and New York. On my first trip I found that one of Puritan's divisions had simply included some of my best dresses in their ordinary range without my label and had not bothered with the others at all.

This was simply a mistake but when Carl heard about it he was furious. All the same I felt I had to spend a couple of days there each week to try to get my things right and prevent my name getting stuck on to designs which had nothing to do with me. I knew it was the intention of those at the top that this should not happen but the company is so huge and its interests are so diversified that mad strange things do happen and nobody appears to know how or anything about them.

I got this way of living on both sides of the Atlantic rather well organized, I think. After two days in the Puritan workrooms, I'd send all the clothes I had with me to the cleaners and travel home with just a small handcase. When I arrived in New York the following week my suite would be full of my familiar clothes all clean and pressed. As it was pretty hot in New York at the time and freezing cold in London, this worked jolly well.

Commuting made me realize what a vast difference there is between working in America and working here. The difference in time was the most difficult thing I had to acclimatize myself to. There is five hours' difference and whenever I needed a drink someone would give me breakfast and, at what felt like breakfast time to me, I was offered a martini.

I was working with three divisions of Puritan ... Young Naturals (which is the sportswear side of the firm), Daphne (junior dresses) and another division which concentrates exclusively on what are called misses' dresses ... which was a great mistake. I had to produce a collection for each one.

Eventually the work was done and I felt reasonably satisfied. But before the first official showing of the clothes I had produced in partnership with Puritan, Alexander and I had to visit Holland. We were to put on a show in an Amsterdam store during British week. We were booked to fly over the day after the historic broadcast of the first colour television to be bounced off Early Bird from London to America. Seven minutes of this programme were filmed in our London flat. We had quite a party there with about fourteen people including Jackie Kennedy's sister Lee Radziwill, Jonathan Miller, Vidal Sassoon, Jon Bannenberg and some of our model girl friends who all turned up loyally wearing my dresses.

We were up till three in the morning seeing this film and doing the live part and we had to catch the seven o'clock plane to Amsterdam. We got there around eight-thirty with our four regular model girls, Sandy, Sarah, Karen and Jan, all feeling pretty terrible. But it was a marvellous day. We spent practically the whole time being photographed. The Dutch had never seen anything like these girls in their short skirts. We made the front page of every single newspaper in Holland the next morning and, subsequently, every single one of their magazines as well.

Then we had to go back to New York. Over there, there are two major fashion market weeks a year and it is during these weeks that all the fashion writers and buyers from over the States converge on the manufacturers who all try desperately to attract the most attention.

Magazines like *Mademoiselle*, *Glamour* and *Seventeen* give vast parties. The biggest one this year was given by *Glamour* and for it they borrowed the name Youthquake from the Puritan company. They had an enormous jazz band. There must have been about four thousand guests and lots of celebrities. Sammy Davis and Sandie Shaw and Dionne Warwick were there and performed and Soupy Sales, who is enormously popular ... a sort of teenage hero ... compèred the whole thing.

Alexander and I sat around with Sally Tuffin and Marion Foale and the four model girls we had with us ... Sandy Moss and Sarah Dawson (who were showing my things) and Patty and Jenny Boyd (who were wearing Tuffin and Foale's clothes) wallowing in the compliments and adulation showered on Britain and the London Look.

There were vast promotion parties every night of the week. Vidal opened his salon on Madison Avenue and gave the best party ever. It was absolutely fantastic ... a real English party with everyone behaving in an extraordinary English way and being rude to each other as only the British can. I think the Americans were simply staggered to see so many eccentric people from this country and so were we! It seemed as if everyone was there ... the pop painters, the pop musicians, everyone you can think of.

After Vidal's party, *Seventeen* gave a gala dinner for us all and we all went on to 'Arthur' – Sylvia Burton's club. It seemed as if the place was completely taken over by the British that night. The Skunks (one of the two regular bands there) composed a special song called 'The Youthquake' and kept on playing it all night. The newspapers were full of the goings-on the next morning.

It wasn't all parties of course. During the day we had to work like mad and I've never had to work in such revolting places as some of those we found ourselves in. Sometimes the conditions were absolutely appalling. And everyone was so rude. We were being bawled at all the time. Sheer brutality flew around in the most extraordinary way. I felt I was working in some ghastly sweated industry.

The girls were superb in spite of all this. They never allowed any onslaught, however rude, to rile them. They put up with everything … not only with the incredible rudeness and the most awful privations, but also with the physical manhandling they got being pushed here, there and everywhere. No one ever seemed to think of saying, 'I wonder if you'd mind coming over here?' or 'Please will you put this on?' They just pushed or shouted.

The girls countered all this with charm and chilly good manners. The Americans couldn't understand. They didn't know how to deal with this kind of exemplary behaviour. Finally they were completely demolished by it and the girls won hands down.

They were absolutely loyal even when totally exhausted by rage and misery. They worked non-stop for ten days being bawled and screamed and shouted at all the time. They were brutally overworked. There was no let-up even for a cup of coffee and a sandwich at any time during the day.

There is another side to the coin of course. There are moments when no one is more generous than an American. Sarah Dawson found this out. Her father was at Las Vegas while we were in New York. He's a great comedian in the Victorian slap-stick manner and was having a terrific success … packing in the audiences. Obviously Sarah was longing for the chance to go and see her father and it did stumble out that she really was awfully homesick. It was almost unbearable for her knowing her father was actually in the States and she couldn't see him. Carl Rosen got wind of this and completely out of the blue a weekend air flight ticket to Vegas arrived from him for Sarah.

So far as living accommodation went, the girls were treated generously. We all stayed at the Algonquin. All their expenses – drinks and everything – were paid for them. And at seven o'clock each morning they were collected from the hotel by a chauffeur-driven Cadillac.

In fact, they had to live at two extremes; on the one hand every comfort and consideration in the few hours they could call their own; on the other, absolute brutality.

They were a sensation in an hotel like the Algonquin of course. One night they all came to our apartment to borrow needles because they'd decided to shorten their dresses still further. Sandy was wearing the most amazing broderie anglaise culottes ... layers upon layers of white frills from the shoulder to five inches above the knee. When we went down to their rooms, the elevator boy was pretty stunned at the sight of her padding along with bare feet in these culottes. So were the couple of people already in the lift. They didn't know whether to smile or just get out quick when, as we walked in, Sarah said, 'Excuse my mother!'

We all managed to have quite a lot of fun. And there were the promotion parties every night. One of the outstanding ones was given by *Seventeen* in the grand ballroom of the Waldorf-Astoria. Sixty models were booked to show the clothes and well over three thousand buyers were invited.

Most of the British designers in New York at the time were there, seated round one large table. With us were Tuffin and Foale, Emmanuelle Khahn and Gerald McCann. From the boxes which are built all the way round the ballroom rather like those in the Albert Hall, we could see people with spy glasses watching us. Quite obviously, they were expecting to see something like Sally Tuffin slapping Gerald McCann and me having a set-to with Marion Foale.

A lot of marvellous young clothes of American design – not like ours but on the same wavelength – were shown, which was terrific. And when our designs came on, we each had to go up on the platform and take a bow. The buyers clapped!

Of course the most important date of all from our point of view was the Puritan company's opening day.

Every manufacturer in New York, whether he has two or four seasons a year, opens with a tremendous party to which all the buyers are invited. Sometimes a few of the Press come too and *Vogue*'s Diana Vreeland turned up at ours which was a terrific honour for she is not much seen in manufacturers' places.

Great banquets of cold meats and caviare and oysters and everything you can think of are laid out and thousands of people come in and out during the day, eating and drinking while the shows go on.

We put on a show every twenty minutes or so. And we did these in exactly the same way as we'd first shown in St Moritz and later developed in the Knightsbridge Bazaar and in Paris. This way of showing is still completely new to American buyers.

We had a six-piece beat group. We managed to get The Skunks from Arthur who are just as way-out in their appearance as anything we've seen here. The boys wear their hair very long and very blond in shades that vary from platinum to brass. The effect is ruined towards the end of the day when you begin to notice the dark stubble trouble they have. However they are good musicians and tough as nails.

About three thousand people – mostly buyers – came in the first day. Alexander and I had to get back to London that night though the girls stayed on to do more shows. We literally fell on the plane. One way and another, it had been a terrifying day and coming at the end of the ten days we'd lived through, we were practically unconscious. But it was all worth it! A week later we had a telephone call to tell us that 50,000 of my dresses had been ordered. And, as a result, Puritan decided it would be worth while to make a colour movie centring round Youthquake and the kind of clothes the first coast-to-coast whistle-stop fashion tour would be showing.

The producer – Michael Margetts – was given a very wide brief. He was simply told to make an eight and a half-minute film that wasn't too commercial promoting the Look.

Nobody really wrote a script. The whole thing was shot over six days. It shows Kari-Ann Moller, Jan de Souza, Geraldine Sinclair and Jenny Boyd in a wild chase against the modern and traditional backgrounds of London to the sound of pop music. They are all wearing Tuffin and Foale's or my clothes. The commercial angle isn't emphasized. The result is very fast-moving and much more like an editorial than an ad. Fifty television stations across the

States have shown this film and it is estimated that, one way or another, something like fifty million people have seen it.

It looked as if everything was set for our Youthquake tour. But there was another battle ahead.

Suddenly Puritan seemed to have a second look at the dollars they'd set aside for the promotion. Suddenly there was a new feeling in the air ... a sort of 'take it easy, fellows' feeling.

It got back to us through rumour and gossip and that kind of thing that the tour wasn't being finalized the way we had planned. To start with, the new idea turned out to be that it was a waste of money to bring model girls out from England. The stores we'd be visiting could fix their own girls. We were supposed to fly in all ready to put on a show ten minutes later with girls who had never seen us before, knew nothing of 'the Look' and might turn out to be any sort of size.

It was an impossible situation. With the itinerary we had ... more than thirty different planes to catch within twenty-one days and God knows how many thousands of miles to cover on deadline timing ... the tour was going to be such hard work that we knew the only way we'd survive would be if we all travelled as one complete unit ... the girls, the clothes, Alexander and I and Paul Young as often as possible. We would have liked our own beat group along with us too but we were quite willing to agree that this wasn't absolutely essential.

I was so worried that suddenly Alexander put his foot down.

'Listen,' he said. 'We can't do a promotion like this, contract or no contract. The only way this tour is workable ... the only way you'll have a promotion worth having ... is if we have our own girls with us who have "the Look", know us, know the clothes, know the way we show them. We've simply got to travel as one complete unit. It is the only way.'

An awful lot of argy-bargy followed but finally it was agreed. And thank God it was. The way things turned out we'd never have got through without Sandy, Sarah and Kari-Ann.

Because they were with us all the time we were able, in the end, to put on a fabulous show at every place. And this in spite of the most awful difficulties. We all know each other so well that the whole thing went over in a thoroughly professional way ... slick as hell ... split-second timing ... the way we've always done our shows.

Sometimes, if we were within reasonable flying distance of New York, The Skunks were able to come out and join us for the day. Other times we'd find a store had managed to get some local pop group ... young boys, some of them still at school, but terrific and so enthusiastic and responsive that they picked up our way of doing things at once. On the whole we didn't have much trouble over the music although at times we arrived at a store to find some crummy old gramophone in one corner of the department which no one had even thought to test for volume.

I've come to the conclusion that the American reputation for super high-powered efficiency is not all it's made out to be. At some of the places we were met with some awful old truck which turned up late at the airport and we'd be taken to some rather ghastly hotel and be expected to dump our personal things and go straight to the store for an early breakfast Press conference. No one seemed to have had the idea that it might be rather a good thing if we were given ten minutes or so for a brush up and since we'd all been up since five in the morning and travelling in the milk plane since six, we could have done with this, particularly the girls who were supposed to arrive immaculately turned out and ready for the photographers.

We'd get another shock when we'd be shown the place where we were supposed to put on the show. In some stores there would be a space cleared in one of the departments probably big enough to take about 250 standing rather uncomfortably tight. We would make a scene but nobody would take the slightest notice of us. They were taken completely by surprise when we got a bit arrogant and said such things as ... Please do it at once ... We've got to have this or that ... The show's due on in ten minutes so you better be quick!

They were completely unprepared and it was only when something like two thousand kids turned up to see the show that they began to get the message.

The thing was that although the buyer had just heard my name because she had been to New York to see the Puritan show and had bought the clothes, it had never really got through to anyone else in the store; no one had any conception of what a show for the young is like; they hadn't thought it worth the trouble to get the things we'd asked for. One of these things was a projector which we needed to show the Youthquake film. A lot of the stores didn't even pretend to bother about this; at others we'd find the projector had been hired but no one had thought to test it on site so often something went wrong.

It was because of all this sort of thing that the first show of the day was always pretty near chaos. We would find the changing rooms for the girls fifty or a hundred yards from a tiny runway and we would all have to scream at everyone in sight until some sort of screens were produced to let the girls do their quick changes near the catwalk. The girls were so keen that I don't think they would have minded particularly if they had had to change in full view of everybody so long as the show kept its pace but the Americans have rather strong ideas on things like this. The Store managers were usually quite polite to me and to Paul and Alexander but they were often bloody to the girls – at least until after the first show.

There were times when the girls really did desperately need a shot in the arm of some kind ... coffee or preferably something stronger ... but we couldn't get it for them. How they got through I'll never know. They were always marvellous and terrific. There was never any sign in the way they showed the clothes of the way they were feeling. However awful everything was ... and it was so awful at times that Alexander was perfectly prepared to pack up and call it a day ... they insisted on going on with the shows. They simply refused to let down the kids who turned up to see them.

Of course once the store had actually seen the effect of some two thousand kids raving and screaming about the clothes, the whole attitude of the place would change. They liked the rush to buy the clothes afterwards, too. In one store five hundred dresses were sold during the day ... it was always between fifty and three hundred sales ... and that's an awful lot of dresses in anybody's language.

Then we'd find lots of people willing to do anything for us. One entire floor of the store would be cleared or, if there was one on the spot, we'd be moved into the auditorium. A few of the more advanced stores are already conscious of the power of the young and they have built on these vast theatres, that hold as many as three thousand, and periodically they hire the local pop group, invite all the youngsters around and provide free entertainment plus a sneaky fashion show.

But nobody seemed to think of putting our show on in a place like this to begin with. They had to be convinced first by the effects of the first one and it was only when they heard the kids raving and shouting and saw the dollar bills coming out of their pockets to buy that the idea occurred to them.

The only thing that counts to the Americans is sales. The whole thing is one hundred per cent commercial; we hadn't really understood this. They are not interested in the young the way we are. This is why they haven't our strength. Young people – like animals – have an instinct about these things. They know we like them and are interested; they know we really want to work for them; we are not only trying to make money.

Some of these kids brought along scrap books to show us ... they'd kept cuttings and photographs of the clothes for ages back. And they brought us little presents ... things they had made themselves and boxes of candies or poems or fruit they had grown at home. Some even turned up in dresses they'd made themselves from designs of mine in the Butterick pattern books and asked me to sign my name on the backs of the dresses.

They were fantastic ... they wanted all our autographs ... Alexander's, Kari-Ann's, Sarah's and Sandy's. Sometimes the local police had to be called in to help keep some sort of order.

I began to feel rather like a Beatle!

We were in a different town every day of the week and in each we had to put on three, four or even five shows. In between these, we'd chat up the local newspapers and magazine people signing autographs while we were talking ... make recordings for the radio ... and shoot over to the television studios to make a film instead of having lunch. At the end of this we'd have to struggle with the packing ... seventy dresses ... fur coats ... all the accessories ... the lot – and get these to the airport ready for a crack of dawn departure the next day. All this in addition to the sixteen pieces of personal luggage we had between us.

Nobody ever got a square meal except perhaps on a Sunday if we were able to catch a plane during the afternoon instead of the morning; and not one of us ever got more than four or five hours' sleep any night.

We had known in advance that it was going to be tough but we had no idea how tough. At the start, Alexander said we'd have to refuse all social invitations ... parties given by presidents of stores and that sort of thing ... simply because we'd need all the sleep we could get. But, curiously, after about ten days of this existence of nothing but work and sleep, we did seem to need some sort of extra life. We began to accept one or two invitations.

At one of these ... a rather good party given by the British Consul in Minneapolis ... a man came up to Kari-Ann and said, 'Goodness, you're beautiful.'

Kari-Ann said, 'Thank you.'

Then he went on, 'What a pity your teeth are not smooth at the tips. They're a bit jagged. As a matter of fact, I'm a dentist. Would you like to come back to my place and I'll fix them for you right away?'

Kari-Ann said, 'How kind. Yes, thank you. I'd love to.'

Then I suppose she had second thoughts. She decided she had better tell us before she disappeared. She said to us, 'I've met this dentist fellow. He thinks my teeth are a bit jagged. He's asked me to go back to his apartment so he can level them off for me. It would be super. Is it all right?'

We were a bit nervous but Kari-Ann went off with him. To our surprise she was back within half an hour with teeth so smooth that there could not have been time for anything else.

I suppose we were rather lucky that we didn't have much trouble with young men trying to get fresh with the girls. I think this is probably due to the fact that the English girls' sophistication is fairly startling to any American who thinks he'd like to have a go.

I've seen the girls give the cold shoulder in a way that must be devastating to the male. I don't really believe that it is possible for an American man to rape an amusing and intelligent English girl ... except by brute force of course. She is far too witty and amusing. She'd simply laugh the whole thing off.

The high spot of the tour was Kansas City though it nearly started off with disaster.

The tour at this stage took us from Chicago to St Louis and from St Louis to Kansas City. Alexander decided he ought to stay over in Chicago the one day we were to be in St Louis to see some knicker manufacturers about the stuff that Youthlines make for us in England. I went on with the girls, the idea being that we'd all meet up again in Kansas City in the evening.

Alexander fell in love with Chicago ... it is a tremendous city ... very beautiful and not a bit like the gloomy, crime-ridden and windy place we'd imagined. I think he left it rather late to catch his plane. Anyway, by the time he was on his way, the most terrific thunderstorm was going on. Apparently the mid-West is racked with turbulent thunderstorms at this time of year. He had an awful flight. He said afterwards he was thankful to be alone, he was so frightened. When he arrived at the Kansas City airport, he found the British Consul there to meet him, who had persuaded the leading radio station (apparently the young listen to the radio over there far more than they ever look at television and only eight per cent of them ever even open a newspaper) to give the day to Britain and all things British. Nothing but British pop music was being played and anyone who took part in the programme was British. He had fixed it that we would take over two and a half hours of the evening programmes.

Alexander became a guest disc jockey under the fatherly eye of a very professional young man who was obviously delighted to have a bit of freedom from the controls and kept disappearing to have a coke or go to the lavatory or some such thing. Most of the time Alexander was alone with a mass of turntables and switches of every possible size controlling something or other and a selection of microphones which were supposed to be used in turn for different effects.

He put on a Beatles record for a start and did a bit of chat about the Beatles pretending we knew them rather better than we do; then he played a few more British records and then suddenly he found he was expected to read the news. He put on a frightfully exaggerated English voice. He started off with a speech of President Johnson's and went on to the weather report. He found he was reading a report on the plane he had just come in on from Chicago. It had caught fire, one engine was burned out but the remaining one had managed to get them to Kansas. A good thing he didn't know at the time!

Then came even more terrifying news. The TWA flight from St Louis was in difficulties. The plane was running through a severe thunderstorm. Alexander knew this was the flight I was on with the girls. He looked out of the window at the top of this small skyscraper that is the local radio station. He could see nothing but thick, low-lying black clouds lit up by lightning such as he'd never seen before. One clap of thunder followed another. He announced that the plane had dropped 20,000 feet and was in real danger.

He had just read the news in fact when I walked into the Control Room. We had had the most awful flight and at one time we were literally turned upside down ... all the girls were terribly sick ... but we got through. I found the Consul's car waiting and I was rushed straight to the radio station.

I joined Alexander for the last ten minutes of the programme.

Next day the store was absolutely packed. We were mobbed. Even Alexander collected his own private fan club as the result of his radio work the day before. He was absolutely delighted – sick of the Mary Quant fans ... he wanted his own!

In a way we think of our time in Kansas City as the pay-off for the whole trip. Literally thousands and thousands of kids turned up for the shows and they were so nice ... so good-looking ... so intelligent ... so inquiring ... that it made all the nightmare worth while. There were so many of them ... they were so in love with our ideas and with the clothes ... they really had done their homework before they came to the show ... they knew all about us and what we were trying to do. They really cared.

And to me – and all of us – this was the most exciting thing in the world.

When Alexander appeared from behind one of the screens he got screamed at!

They loved the short, short skirts. They would have liked theirs as short as Kari-Ann's but schools don't approve! I don't think anybody except perhaps the very, very young will ever dare to cut their skirts as short as we do. I know we were looked at as a pretty odd-looking bunch. The Americans have no inhibitions. Complete strangers would come up to us … sometimes a whole string of them … in hotel lobbies and at the airports and say something like, 'What are you? What are you doing here? How extraordinary you look.'

Finally Sandy, who's a wit, got fed up with saying, 'We're a fashion group. This is Mary Quant,' and started saying, 'We're the latest pop group from London. We're The Junket Creams!'

The name stuck!

We had to have police protection to get us back to our hotel in Kansas City. Not that we wanted to be protected from the girls but we would never have got through the streets without it. And when we arrived, we found that about sixty of them had beaten us to it. They were already in the foyer fighting off the concierge or bell boy Captain or whatever he's called insisting that they were not going to leave until we arrived. We took a whole lot of them up to our rooms. They wanted to know everything. They may have appeared star-struck with all their screaming and raving but they were very intelligent girls as well.

They absolutely bombarded us all with questions … they lapped up anything we could tell them about London. They asked … what is it like to work in the fashion trade over here? … do all the girls look like Kari-Ann and Sarah and Sandy? … what are the Beatles really like? … and the Rolling Stones? How does one start being a designer? … why does everything happen first in London now and not in Paris? … why doesn't anything happen first in America? … if they ever managed to get to England, where should they go? … could they ring us up and would we give them introductions to the exciting people here?

Those who had already visited London had the chance to be wonderfully superior and they took full advantage of it!

They were all mad about the Vidal Sassoon haircut; in the end we all had pairs of scissors and did our best to imitate Vidal. A good thing he wasn't there to see us! But the kids loved it. The floor was knee-deep in golden hair by the time we'd finished. Fortunately we were getting out of town on the milk plane the next morning.

Back to New York. There was some consolation in knowing that the whole thing had been a success. I knew it had been a success simply because every single one of us had felt all the time that each was responsible for making it so. We'd been living in each other's pockets for three and a half weeks and we'd never had a row. No one had ever been late for a plane. We hadn't lost one single thing. But we were worn to a shred.

We sat down to the first decent dinner we'd had in weeks after what was probably the toughest day of the lot but at least we had come to the end of the tour. There was nothing to worry about the next morning.

It was then we had our first row!

The battle was over so I suppose we all let go and got all the pent-up emotions of the past weeks out of the system. It really was extraordinary.

The next day we went off to Boston to spend the week-end with Carl.

Paul Young knows that I love riding in small planes and helicopters and he'd made a special effort to surprise me. When we got to the airport we found a tiny plane waiting for us. I sat up front with the pilot, Alexander and Paul behind me and Sandy somewhere in the tail.

We came down on a tiny runway near Boston … not an airport, just a few huts and masses of tiny planes flying around. From the plane we could see Carl waiting for us. This was terrific. This was wonderful! This really surprised us! We didn't really feel we'd had that much success!

He came rushing over before we untied our seat belts.

'Shirley' (that's his wife) 'has gone off to the beach with the children. We're going to join her there.'

He leapt into the plane, ignoring the little 'no smoking' sign. He sat down, still puffing away; he punched the pilot on the back.

'Never seen you before,' he said. 'I suppose you know the way?'

'Where is it you want to go?' he asked.

Carl replied, 'I don't know what you call it. It's somewhere over by the beach near Falmouth. I've some cars waiting for us there.'

'What sort of landing is there ... a sort of airstrip?'

'Yeah ... yeah,' said Carl. 'It's a field. I think it's about a hundred yards long. What sort of plane is this? Can you land in a hundred yards?'

The pilot sort of gulped. 'Well ... yeah ... I think we might. We'll have a go. Trees at the end or anything like that?'

'Sure. Plenty of trees.'

Suddenly Carl seemed to become aware of Alexander who really was a bit green round the gills.

'Don't worry,' Carl said. He turned to the pilot again.

'Look, I don't want you to take any risks. You can take risks when my contract with these people runs out. For the next few years, this girl's going to be rather valuable to me. You'll find an air force base about ten miles further up the coast. Go there. Radio the other place and ask the cars to meet us.'

So we made it. The cars were waiting and we went off to join Shirley on the beach. We spent the day bathing and yachting and all the rest of it. I went back to Boston in the plane and had a super time because the pilot let me take over the controls and I actually landed the thing.

Alexander had had enough of flying for one day. He went back in one of the cars.

Carl's house is a huge affair on the outskirts of Boston. Alexander and I were given the beach house. There's no beach. It's a sort of super luxurious shack on the edge of a huge swimming pool, absolutely self-contained with a kitchen and refrigerator and air conditioning and all the rest of it.

We spent all our time in the pool with Carl's children who are sweet and hadn't had much chance of playing with grownups before. We went swimming with them; we had fights with them; and we built all sorts of extraordinary things together. We got infantile ourselves for the week-end.

And all the time we were playing these nonsense games with the kids, Carl was sitting on the edge of the pool close to a pink telephone ... very tanned ... very handsome ... holding up a sun reflector so that he'd get the maximum out of every minute ... his chief accountant beside him, also in very smart bathing trunks, his hands full of papers covered with figures.

Back in New York, we had four days in which to launch the second Puritan collection to the Press, do some radio work and make some television, particularly the Merv Griffin show, before we went back to London.

The Press launch went off beautifully. The Americans seem to love shows at nine o'clock in the morning with elaborate breakfasts. The Skunks were with us but everyone was feeling far too ill and headachy for music of any kind at the start.

When breakfast was over, we ran through the Youthquake film. As it ended, a curtain was drawn back at one end of the room and The Skunks started playing rather quietly.

On the stage were four very camp beds with an antique telephone beside each one. In each bed was a girl with the bedclothes pulled right up to her nose, lying flat on her back, her glossy boots sticking out over the end.

One by one the telephones went off. One by one the girls woke up, terribly sleepy and rubbing their eyes and yawning. Suddenly they all leapt out of bed; they were wearing the new clothes.

This gave the show just the right kind of kick-off. Everybody laughed like mad and decided to enjoy themselves. The applause was such as I have never heard before from Press people, who don't applaud easily. The mood of the whole thing was right. And the girls were right ... from their haircuts to the toes sticking out of their boots.

It was a terrific show. Tuffin and Foale were there and two young American designers who are also in on this Youthquake thing of Puritan's. It worked marvellously.

The more of us there are, the better it will always work. No one person can put over a new philosophy. There has got to be support from others. We are all different but, in a sense, we're all taking bites from the same apple. We are all aiming at the same thing but at different parts of the target. Whatever one of us does will help the others.

When the show was over, the girls went up on the roof to be filmed for the Merv Griffin show. There was another thunderstorm so they had to dance about in the rain.

Afterwards the *New York Herald Tribune* photographers came backstage. They jostled into the girls' dressing-room and found them lying flat on the floor absolutely out. This was the picture the photographers took. It appeared next morning. I thought it was rather good because it put over far better than any ordinary fashion photograph could have done, the terrific pace and impact and the fantastic effort these girls have to make to translate the mood into visual fact.

All the way back to London in the plane we tortured each other with all the crises and disasters we knew would be waiting for us. We had never been away from the office, the workrooms and the showroom and shops for so long before.

Imagine our chagrin to find that everything was going swimmingly. Archie and all the people who work with us were completely in control and, to add insult to injury, someone in the workroom asked me if I had enjoyed my holiday. However, even this was capped by great Aunt Flora, who asked Alexander's mother, 'When is he going to get a proper job?'

INDEX

Mary Quant is MQ and Alexander Plunkett Greene is APG throughout.